Be a
BIG TIME, BIG DEAL
Private Eye

RUSS BUBAS
PALADIN PRESS

Be a
BIG TIME, BIG DEAL
Private Eye

**. . . and Make Money at It
in Today's Business World**

Be a Big Time, Big Deal Private Eye
. . . and Make Money at It in Today's Business World
by Russ Bubas

Copyright © 2017 by Russ Bubas

ISBN: 978-1-945756-16-0
Published by Merrimack Media,
665 Washington St., #2507
Boston, Massachsuetts

Direct inquiries and/or orders to the above address.

Front cover photo: ©iStockphoto.com/Gord Horne
Back cover photo: ©iStockphoto.com/Olivier Blondeau

CONTENTS

In troduction

"When you're slapped, you'll take it and like it!"
—Sam Spade
The Maltese Falcon

In the early days of the United States, the image of the Western lawman was born. Independent, competent, tough, with his own set of ethics and morals, the sheriff of the Old West became the quintessential image of America around the world. The country matured, but the myth of the Western lawman has stayed with our culture to this day. It's part of our DNA.

As a natural evolution of this uniquely American figure came the modern-day version, the private investigator. Like the sheriff, the myth held that he was independent and resourceful, sometimes operating on the fringe of the law, but generally dedicated to a higher moral good. Instead of his faithful horse, he drove a sports car or convertible, usually of dubious reliability and behind in the payments. Instead of the six-shooter at his hip, he had a tape recorder in his pocket and possibly a .38 in a shoulder holster. We've seen this mutation with the likes of Philip Marlowe, Sam Spade, and Mike Hammer, and sometimes the tough guy is softened into an intellectual Spenser, Peter Gunn, or Rockford. Although the grit may vary, the prototype remains the same—smart, tough, even glamorous.

What was once a fascinating cultural footnote has become an increasingly important player in the modern business world. Today's successful private eye is a sophisticated Internet traveler, even a shrewd businessman and corporate executive. It would now be rare indeed to find a private investigator with a whiskey bottle in his bottom drawer, a moon-eyed, sexy secretary ready to serve his every whim, and the impression of a keyhole fixed firmly over his right eye. But the heritage remains.

Of course, some of that heritage is not stellar. Like the Western lawmen, some private eyes became known for their sleazy and sometimes illegal actions. This lends spice and color to the legend, but now, instead of being on the fringe, the private investigator in 21st century America fills a critical and ever-increasing role, often filling gaps where regular law enforcement cannot or will not tread, either due to lack of resources, lack of interest, or restrictive laws. The old stigma of the gum-shoed sleaze, willing to do any dirty thing for a small price, has disappeared, replaced by an enormously diverse industry serving a wide variety of purposes—some great, some not so great, and some indifferent.

This book will describe the more common (and not so common) slices of the private investigation business, including who uses these services and why. Most importantly, it will help you make money at it if you decide to enter the profession. And along the way, we will try not to lose sight of the cachet, adventure, and satisfaction found in the PI business. After all, what fun is it if you can't spin stories at cocktail and dinner parties?

Ch apter 1
Shopping
Services

Posing as an ordinary customer to uncover employee theft, dishonesty, and poor performance falls under the broad category of shopping services. Sometimes viewed as the bottom of the service barrel, shopping services are nonetheless a great way to hone investigative skills, get your business organized, and, most importantly, make yourself visible to potential clients.

DETECTING CASH THEFT

As mom-and-pop stores grew into chains and pop hired people other than mom to run the cash register, a need to detect and eliminate theft at the point of sale was created. That's when spotters, checkers, and shoppers were born—people hired by the storeowner to act as ordinary customers but whose job was to inconspicuously monitor employees for dishonest or illegal behavior. Indeed, demand for this service was so high that private investigators became as familiar with the old NCR cash registers as they are with computers today.

Cashiers, handling other people's money, can easily and quickly learn how to "clip" a sale; that is, collect money from a customer for a legitimate sale and either fail to ring it into the register or under ring it (i.e., enter an amount less than what the item cost) so that some or all of the money wouldn't reflect in the total amount collected that day. This creates an overage of cash in the register, which can be slipped into a pocket, sock, or bra to increase the pay of the smug, grinning employee. Savvy companies soon learned to eliminate pockets in aprons and other uniforms just to slow down these misappropriations, but ingenious employees found a variety of other hiding spots, such as tip cups and even inside the register frame itself. The more clever of these register thieves would place the money into the register drawer but keep track of how much was under rung, then remove the excess cash when the opportunity presented itself, usually just before quitting time.

Cashiers with three-digit IQs could keep track of the amount of money they clipped in their head, but the average dunderhead had to do so in some other way. A variety of methods were invented, such as placing pennies in one of the register slots each time a sale was not rung up, doing the same with toothpicks, or even stupidly writing down what was going to be stolen on a pad next to the register. (This happened more often than you would think.)

One of the more tricky ways of keeping track, used by bartenders, was to keep a plastic swizzle stick in their mouth, like a toothpick. Every time a sale was not rung up, they would bite the stick, placing a small indentation in it. Count up the indentations at the end of the night, and you know how much extra is in the register. If you think about it, you've probably seen a swizzle stick in more than one bartender's mouth.

Bar owners who let their bartenders read the registers and calculate sales totals for the day quickly found themselves out of business—often looking at the new bar across the street, opened by their former trusted employee. We once found a bartender who brought in his own cash register to ring up some of the sales. Since none of those sales were included in the daily audits, he kept all the money rung into that register. When we reported that the bartender rung up the sales on register three, the owner said, "What register three?" and finally realized what was happening.

Owners of bars, restaurants, convenience stores, retail shops, and practically any business that collected cash hired private eyes to spot-check their cashiers and catch them not ringing sales, thereby stealing cash from them. In fact, such large investigation and security companies as Dale Systems, Merit, and Wackenhut started out by checking cashiers locally and grew into national

4

operations, with investigators constantly on the road, going from location to location, posing as customers, and making "buys" from potentially dishonest cashiers.

Drugstore chains, convenience store chains, and restaurants were important first users of this investigative service. Movie theaters, starting back when matinees cost a nickel, were also an important early client. Theater owners would hire a private eye to go into a particular show as a patron and count heads with a palmed counter. The number of patrons counted was then compared to the cash take for that showing. More heads than cash meant someone had their hand in the till.

So, how did PIs catch dirty employees at this game? Basically, they would pose as customers, make cash sales, and watch how the money was handled. These cash "drops" were made in a special way to provide the opportunity for a cashier to not record the sale. For example, the investigator would make exact cash payment for an item and walk away without waiting for a receipt, but he would remember a series of sales before his and make note of the exact time of his sale. The owner would then review the journal details of the register to verify if the investigator's sale was or was not there. Often, detectives worked in teams of two—one making the drop sale and walking away; the other, several feet away or in line, watching to see if the sale was rung up properly. (Today, clients can look up suspicious transactions on point-of-sale journal tapes, so it's still important to get a series of sales before and after the questionable sale, along with exact times, to make that research possible and relatively easy.)

Another method used by slick PIs was called the double buy. An item would be purchased and a large bill presented for payment, such as a $20 bill for a $5 purchase. When the cashier rung up the item and as change was being made from the open cash drawer, the investigator would pick up another item for purchase and tell the cashier to take payment from the change. Now the cashier had two choices: either close the cash drawer and ring up the second item properly, or simply take payment from the change, ring up nothing, and spirit this little treasure into his pocket. Thousands of dishonest employees were caught with this method.

Detecting dishonest cashiers and bartenders often becomes a hilarious cat-and-mouse game. As a young and eager spotter, I was sent into the wilds of New York City bars to check as many as possible. Sometimes this meant visits to five or more bars in a day, purchasing at least two drinks in each. This often led to completely illegible notes and tape recordings, not to mention all the trouble just getting home.

Cleverly, I decided I would use a rubber syringe ball pirated from a squirting flower trick. The idea was to order a drink without mix, suck up the booze from the glass when no one was looking, and secrete the rubber ball, now filled with scotch or whatever, into my pocket. It looked good on paper.

So, on assignment, I sidled into a bar on Canal Street, about three o'clock in the afternoon. The denizens of this questionable establishment consisted of a bartender the size of the Hulk, one apparent Hells Angel, and two or three members of the perpetually drunk. Of course I, in my chinos and button-down oxford, thought that I fit right in.

Inconspicuously seating myself in front of the glaring bartender, I ordered a scotch, neat. The bartender filled a rocks glass to the brim and plopped it in front of me without a word. Using my best detective peripheral vision, I craftily checked out the clientele and, when I thought the time was right, levered my palm, in which was concealed my secret weapon, over the glass of scotch. With a barely audible slurp, I sucked up the contents.

Slyly looking around to see if anything was noticed, it looked like all were still staring into their respective glasses and I was home free. Then, glancing at my glass, I discovered only half the scotch was gone. Waiting a respectable time, I again palmed my rubber ball and tried to suck up the remainder. What I didn't figure out was that when I squeezed the ball to suck up the rest, what was in the ball came rushing out in a torrent, squirting into the glass and blowing up in my face.

Trying to look inconspicuous with my face and shirt covered in scotch was very, very difficult. It became even more difficult when a being seated down the bar, whom I had figured for a zombie when I entered, screamed, "Holy shit! His drink blew up! His drink blew up!" Then, "I'll have one of those!"

My money was already on the bar. I tried desperately to think of a reason why I was suddenly drenched with Mr. Dewar's finest. Spontaneously exploding scotch did not seem reasonable, so I slinked out with burning eyes behind me.

Over the years I killed countless plants by dumping drinks, and occasionally I would pour a drink into a styrene bag kept in my pocket, then unload the contents in the rest room later. I've had bartenders yell at me, point out my feeble disguises, and offer me money for good reports. However, by doggedly providing this investigative service, I got clients, and that led to other clients. And, significantly, I got my feet wet.

MYSTERY SHOPPER

The lion's share of shopping services today is comprised of a service called the mystery shopper, and it has more to do with customer service than with missing money. Retailers and hospitality people live in a fiercely competitive world, where word of mouth can be deadly and customer service rules. One of the most effective ways for a business to evaluate quality of service is through random spot checks by private investigators posing as customers. Not only does it identify problems and ascertain attitudes of the workforce, it is a terrific deterrent against bad service, as each customer ends up being treated like a spotter by the employees who fear that he or she is one.

The downside of this evolution is that you don't need to be a licensed private eye to do mystery spots for customer service. That's why literally thousands of housewives, retired people, and part-timers are now in the business. Further, there are national databases that list tens of thousands of full- and part-time mystery shoppers. Let's face it: how many people love to shop and get paid for it? In fact, most of this business is now done not by investigators but by market-research firms, who draw on this pool of ordinary folks to do the legwork in the field.

A niche for private investigators still exists, however, and it goes back to the old days: watching for cash being clipped at the point of sale. This is a valuable service to any business that collects cash from customers, which means that your potential client base still includes movie theaters, bars, restaurants, convenience stores, amusement facilities, retail outlets, and any other business where money changes hands on the premises. And it is a specialized skill that cannot be performed by your average mystery shopper.

For a beginning PI, this is a great place to start because it's relatively easy to get business and can lead to additional work. For example, if the fledgling detective approaches a bar owner and proposes to "spot" a bartender and is good enough to detect that he is not ringing sales, the client may very well want to know how long the bartender has been dirty and how much money he's taken, which leads to an interview/interrogation for the PI. Or the client may be interested in checking out the next bartender or manager he hires, so he'll want a background investigation. Often the client wants to know what happens at closing time and beyond, which means a surveillance.

The PI needs to approach each mystery shop not as a "shop" but as a mini-investigation, keeping in mind that the most mundane inspection can lead to a major case. I once caught a bartender placing a $5 bill that belonged in the register into his tip cup instead. After reasoning with him during a subsequent interview, he returned more than $77,000 in cash the next day—money he'd clipped from the bar that he was setting aside for his retirement house in Florida.

A smart way to generate additional business for yourself is to approach a potential client with the suggestion of detecting integrity issues, then providing customer service and operational information along with it. While posing as a customer and watching sales being rung up, the enterprising PI can also provide information on courtesy, cleanliness, customer comments or complaints, and all things important to the owner. The best way to go about this is to pretend the establishment is yours and determine what you would want to know—good, bad, or ugly.

Above all, shopping inspections for theft provide an enormous benefit that is often overlooked: just as with customer service mystery shops, they are a strong deterrent against improper behavior. I've had clients tell me that they wish to stop ongoing inspections because no one had been caught in a while. I point out that that is exactly why they should not stop the surveys. Employees know they are being spot-checked and are more inclined to follow policy, because they never know when the person on the other side of the counter is an investigator posing as a regular customer. The shopping inspection is really a control that *prevents* theft and losses.

REPORTING

Reports that provide the findings of a shopping service investigation have changed and streamlined over the past computer-driven years. The original method, and probably still the best, is a narrative report, generally organized chronographically from start to finish. (See Appendix A.) Sometimes the important findings will be summarized at the beginning of the report and then fleshed out in the body. Violations of established policy should always be highlighted. You can never provide too much detail, and the gospel of answering "who, what, when, where, why, and how" should always be followed. Nothing irritates a client more than to have *more* questions after he gets the report than before.

When completing a narrative report for shopping services, the investigator should again ask himself what would be deemed important if he were the owner. In other words, put yourself in the driver's seat and report on what you would want to know about your own business. Start with that and add what the real owner feels is important. Just some of the areas you could cover with a customer service inspection include:

- Were employees working in an efficient manner? If not, describe what they were or were not doing.
- Was service fast and courteous? How fast (or slow) was it? Be specific. If it took 25 minutes to receive your meal, state that.
- Were employee appearances in accordance with policy? If not, how were they not?
- Was the establishment clean? If not, give specific details.

While you obviously need to detail any problems encountered by you or other customers, also include any positive actions or observations. The shopping inspection is not just about finding derogatory things but to provide a mini supervisory audit of the operation, so it should point out the good as well as the bad. Objectivity and accuracy, as in any investigative report, are crucial. If you think you observed something but are not sure, you can still report it, but you should qualify it with phrases like, "It appeared" or "Observations indicated" to get information across that is not or cannot be verified.

Check-off reports are becoming more and more popular, especially for customer service inspections. (See Appendix B.) First, they are fast and easy to read. Secondly, the client is not overwhelmed with paper. Thirdly, they are easy to transmit electronically. Lastly, and most importantly (especially for large chains), they are conducive to summaries and comparisons. By answering the same questions for different locations, you are able to compare one to another. You can even weight the questions to arrive at a numerical score and then calculate percentages for various locations. Companies often factor these reports in when determining bonuses for management.

Investigators for modern shopping service companies, especially those specializing in customer service inspections, will often touch in a report on a personal digital assistant (PDA) such as a BlackBerry immediately after doing the inspection. This is sent electronically to a central clearing location, edited, and forwarded immediately to the client. In this way, clients can receive reports from a shopping inspection within minutes after the mystery survey is done. This kind of instantaneous reporting is like having additional on-site supervisors at a fraction of the cost.

The reporting format can largely be left up to the client, but you'll find that the smaller companies will be happy to accept what you feel is best for them, while the larger, more experienced chains usually will have their own reporting format already determined. In either case, it's always good business to try to modify each report for each client. Customized reports are a good way to maintain the business. Ask for the client's operations manual, and formulate good questions to answer based on documented policies and procedures. Then develop a report that hits the target and becomes an indispensable tool for management.

Regardless of which format you use, certain points of information should always be included. For integrity reports:

- Always give transactional information, such as check or transaction number, amount of the transaction, and employee name or number. This allows the client to look up and verify the transaction.
- Give the date, day of the week, and exact time—again, so the client can verify the transaction.

- Give detailed descriptions of the employee and his/her appearance.
- Identify management personnel and describe their actions.
- Report any violations of policy, such as open register drawers, packages in and around points of sale, etc.
- List any incorrect prices.
- Describe any outside people of a suspicious nature, including their appearance, activities on the premises, and interactions with employees.

For customer service inspections:

- Describe the greeting and length of time before it's received.
- Report on courtesy and employee demeanor to patrons.
- Report any suggestive selling (i.e., suggesting additional items to a customer, such as appetizers, wine, or desserts, to pump up the check).
- Describe the cleanliness and orderliness of the location.
- Repeat the closing salutation, if any.
- Mention any customer complaints or comments.
- Report in detail any problems observed.

PRICING AND PROFITABILITY

Making money on mystery shopping inspections is decidedly a mixed bag. If you're getting started and you are able to land a handful of mom-and-pop type accounts, you'll find you will not be making much in the way of profit. You can charge single-location bar owners between $75 and $95 per visit, plus reimbursement for the money you spend on their behalf in their location. Today, getting more than $100 per inspection is tough, but that will probably change soon. Also, clients will expect a flat fee arrangement that includes your travel time. Factoring in travel expenses can kill your margin. On the other hand, if you can establish a pool of clients who are grouped close to each other geographically, you can cut that expense drastically.

Chain stores can be quite lucrative if you can cut through the home-office bureaucracy and establish a relationship with them. Even convenience stores—for which you'll be hard pressed to get more than $25 to $40 per inspection—can be profitable when you can visit multiple locations in a single day. Even at $25 per inspection, in-and-out surveys of convenience stores close by may provide for 8 to 10 inspections in a day. That's $250 or so in a day, a living wage.

Hotels will pay from $350 to $1,200 or more for check-ins with full property inspections. This is an inspection where you survey all guest services, providing reports on the parking valet, concierge, front desk personnel, bellman service, and room service, as well as any food and beverage outlets on site. Finally, the condition and contents of the room are critiqued. This is a lot of reports, but you could do two or three properties in a week. Again, a living wage.

Some high-end national hotel chains do extensive mystery shops, having the inspectors stay on the property for two or more days. Experts in this business, usually former hoteliers themselves, may charge as much as $5,000 per visit. However, these are extremely detailed surveys and are so important that they are often tied to that hotel's rating.

The following is a list of price parameters for mystery shopping services. These are general guidelines, accurate at the time of this book's publication, that may or may not have any bearing on what you charge your client. A rule of thumb to determine your fee (unless dictated by your dreaded competition) is to figure out how much time you will need to spend to do a good survey, then make sure you get at least $45 to $50 per hour for your time.

- Bars and restaurants—$50 to $95 per visit, generally half the second fee when doing a bar/restaurant together.
- Retail stores—$35 to $65 per visit, the higher fee if checking fitting rooms or returns.
- Convenience stores—$25 to $40 per visit, usually depending on locations.
- Movie theaters—$35 to $45 for straight survey, $45 or more if providing head counts.
- Banks—$30 to $50 per visit, higher if checking loan procedures, etc.
- Auto dealerships—$85 to $125 per visit.

There are certain things you can do to protect your profit:

▸ Determine your travel distance and, if unreasonably far, request to be compensated for mileage at somewhere around $.50 per mile. Try to get full travel in every case.

▸ Tell your client that your flat fee is based on a certain amount of time. For example, a standard bar shop should take between 45 minutes to an hour. Additional payment for time spent beyond that should be figured on an hourly basis or a multiple of your flat fee.

▸ If returning merchandise purchased as part of the inspection, make sure you are compensated properly.

▸ Transmit your reports via e-mail or Web-based communication rather than through the mail.

▸ Make sure your client understands that there are additional charges for extra services such as interrogations, testifying in court, and so forth. These are normally billed on an hourly basis, and the fee structure may be different than the fee for the inspection.

▸ Make sure your client does not terminate an employee or take other action on the basis of one report. Insist that violations of policy be verified by two or more observations.

Years ago, I thought that with the advent of sophisticated point-of-sale electronics, the mystery shopper would go the way of hula hoops and eight-track tapes. But I underestimated the ingenuity of crooked people handling other people's money. Even with POS terminals and scanners, there is still a need for these kinds of spotting and audit surveys. When coupled with the customer service information that vicious competition requires, the intelligence gathered through this service can be very valuable to the right client.

Many PIs ignore this field of investigation, or fail to understand how to make it a part of their arsenal. Mystery shopping may be considered the bottom rung of the private investigation case ladder, but for a young, entry-level investigator starting out without large capital or contacts, it can be the best way to get going. It takes work and perseverance, but it can open the door to additional clients and other investigative services.

Chapter 2
Background Investigations and Employee Screenings

Any new employee should come to work with a solid background of integrity and character, be honest and sincere with the prospective employer, and not be deceptive in any way. Verifying this can absolutely be the best loss-prevention action an employer can take—and this is where the private investigator, with solid work and common sense, can be so valuable.

It has always seemed incredible to me that so many employees get hired without a background check. If you calculate costs vs. rewards, the formula goes something like this:

> ▶ If you hire an employee at $25,000 a year, with FICA and other taxes, benefits, and perks, he or she costs the company at least $30,000 the first year and every year thereafter. This does not take into account pay raises.
>
> ▶ If a background investigation costs $100, the cost of knowing whom you are hiring is one three-hundredth of that person's first year's salary. This makes it by far the most cost-effective loss-prevention action a company can take and is by far the cheapest insurance.

Furthermore, corporate security studies have shown that:

- Employee theft is estimated to cost businesses $50 billion per year.

- 33 percent of new business failures are due to employee theft.
- 33 percent of all job applicants lie on their application.
- 5 percent falsify their name, Social Security number, or driver's license information.
- There are approximately 11,000 instances of work-place violence each year, costing an average of $250,000 per incident.

Now compare that grim picture to these figures:

- A good background check will reduce shrinkage (i.e., inventory shortages) by 93 percent.
- A good background check will reduce turnover by 72 percent.
- A good background check will improve productivity by 51 percent.

With information like this, you can make a good case for a potential client to hire you to do employee screenings.

Companies that specialize in background investigations often define themselves as "consumer reporting agencies" rather than investigative agencies. The difference is subtle but important. Some of the privacy statutes governing the collection and dissemination of personal background information clearly acknowledge the distinction and place additional controls over private investigators rather than "reporting services." The private investigator can get around this by establishing a spin-off company that serves strictly as a consumer reporting agency and does not conduct other investigations. In actuality, one hand washes the other.

SOLVING CASES WITH BACKGROUND CHECKS

The president of a nonprofit retail chain asked me to try to find out who stole more than $5,000 from the main store's safe. Considering there was no evidence of forced entry, and being a trained detective, I asked the insightful question, "Who has access to the combination?"

Turned out, only three people: the general manager and two assistant managers. That was a start. I then asked if background checks had been done on any of the three individuals. Nothing had been done (no surprise), so I made that my first action.

Nothing came up with the two assistants, but the general manager had listed on his application that he had been operating a photography business for seven years in New York state. This was odd, as the employment he listed did not jibe with his previous residences. Another question arose: how did he go from running a photography business to managing a charity retail store?

Digging further, it turned out that he was not really running a photography business but was taking photography lessons while incarcerated at Attica State Prison. Even worse, he was incarcerated for chopping up his baby son with a machete while under the influence of PCP. Digging a little deeper, I learned that he was in fact still on parole, so I called his parole officer. He was fairly candid:

"If anything bad happened, he probably did it. He's a really bad guy."

The company had absolutely no knowledge of this and never bothered to check his background or even look at his application.

I went to his office, sat down, and told him what I found and even what his parole officer had said. I then told him that, obviously, he was my primary suspect. He just smiled, took out the keys to the store, placed them on the desk, put on his jacket, and walked out, never to return to the job.

I called the president and told him what I learned from my background investigation and what had happened during the interview, and that, logically, I felt I had figured out who had taken the money. Turned out that the background check was better than searching for fingerprints, conducting interrogations, or anything else. If it had been done when the manager was hired, chances are the five grand would have never been lost, not to mention whatever else that was never discovered.

Similar incidents have occurred countless times in countless companies, yet it took the horror of the terrorist attacks on September 11, 2001, to increase awareness of the importance of background checks to an unprecedented level. Prior to 9/11, many companies winked at the pre-employment screening function, interested more in filling spots than in screening who was filling those spots. Even though all good businesspeople agreed about the importance of doing background investigations, it was often performed haphazardly and inconsistently, and it was mostly left up to human resource people who had little expertise in the techniques of employee screening. After 9/11, hiring managers realized that people looking to do harm could be in their midst, and they now wanted to know if the new engineer was spending vacation time at some undisclosed location on the Pakistani frontier. (The thinking wasn't restricted to potential terrorists—it also included people who might steal, do drugs, etc.) In a sense, September 11 was a blow to naiveté.

The heightened awareness after 9/11 spawned new and streamlined services. Information resellers have designed programs for employee screening that are quick, relatively thorough, and very inexpensive. Companies such as ChoicePoint sell packages that enable employers to do their own background checks at very low cost—costs that individual investigators cannot meet. This is not to say there is still not a niche for the small agency or independent investigator to profit in this area; indeed, personalized service along with insightful investigative logic and perception can create a very nice business for investigators skilled in the art of background investigations. But any high volume of employee screenings is now monopolized by the big database resellers. (More on this below.)

PRE-EMPLOYMENT SCREENINGS

The most basic background service is screening prospective employees. This is generally the highest volume—and lowest margin—work. A pre-employment screening must be done in a timely manner and, most importantly, the PI must be able to give the client definition of and insight into the facts found.

The investigator providing this service must understand the need for flexibility in the depth of the report (i.e., match the job description and the risk it entails with the detail of the applicant's history) and price accordingly. For example, a bartender may only require a narrow report (credit and criminal records), while the bar manager would require a full report (identity verification, credit and criminal records, employment history, motor vehicle records, education verification, etc.). Tailoring the depth of the report (and therefore the price) is a nice selling point to a prospective client. The PI should be able to provide clear recommendations in that regard, but, of course, the ultimate decision is up to the client. You may feel that a key-holding manager should have a full background done, while your client may think a criminal records check is enough.

A standard (full) report for an important new employee, such as a manager or cashier, generally includes the following:

Identity Verification

This is done through what's called a "credit report header," which will verify identity through Social Security number and provide any aliases by which the person is known. Getting a credit header is the first thing to do and is very inexpensive. After you have been doing this for a while, you will be stunned how many people you will find living under aliases and/or who have false or multiple Social Security numbers. We've encountered people living under false identities, concealing past incarcerations, even hiding out in the witness protection program. We had one guy, a high-level project manager, who changed his name to hide the fact that he faked his own death to get out of paying back federal loans.

Credit Reports

All good background checks start with a credit report. The credit report not only shows if the applicant pays his bills on time, it also shows the amount of financial pressure he or she is under. This can be a gauge for risk for handling money. Individuals under a heavy financial burden who are having trouble making payments can be very tempted to take advantage of their position to ease the pressure they are facing.

Even more important, the credit report provides insight into the applicant's character. If his life is in shambles—not meeting payments, overspending, etc.—chances are his performance in the new job will be the same.

Access to and use of credit reports is strictly regulated by the Fair Credit Reporting Act and can only be done for permissible purposes. The 10 permissible purposes—which you should *never* violate—are:

1. As ordered by a court or grand jury subpoena.
2. In response to the written request of the consumer.
3. In connection with a credit transaction, such as extending credit, or the review or collection of a consumer's account.
4. For employment purposes, including hiring and promotion decisions, where the consumer has given written permission.
5. For the underwriting of insurance as a result of an application from a consumer.
6. When there is a legitimate business need, in connection with a business transaction that is initiated by the consumer.
7. To review a consumer's account to determine whether the consumer continues to meet the terms of the account.
8. To determine the consumer's eligibility for a license or other benefit granted by a governmental instrumentality required by law to consider an applicant's financial responsibility or status.
9. For use by a potential investor or servicer, or current insurer, in a valuation or assessment of the credit or prepayment risks associated with an existing credit obligation.
10. For use by state or local officials in connection with the determination of child support payments, or modifications and enforcement thereof.

Number four is the justification used by agencies to conduct pre-employment screenings and background investigations. To pull credit records for a pre-employment screening, you need a signed release from the applicant. (See Appendix C.) It is not enough that the applicant signed the bottom of the employment application acknowledging that the job may be contingent on a background check—a separate notification form is required to get a credit report.

Reading a credit report can be akin to deciphering the Dead Sea Scrolls, but any credit bureau can give you an interpretation of the symbols and abbreviations. After awhile, you'll learn exactly how to recognize solid credit as well as the red flags that indicate shaky finances or character. Interpreting the report for your client is where you really earn your fee—if you discover, for instance, that the applicant is behind on payments for a number of weekends at the Mammoth Hotel and Casino in Las Vegas, you could point out that there might be a gambling problem to consider.

It is still possible to review a credit report in conjunction with an investigation, but be aware that the credit bureaus are required to list a notification on the report indicating who pulled the records, which could blow a confidential investigation.

Essentially, the credit report provides the backbone of any background check. Even when the client only wants a check of criminal records, try to pull the credit report, too. Although a little more difficult to obtain due to compliance laws, it is very inexpensive and can provide even better insight into the prospective employee's suitability for the position.

Criminal Records

Criminal records are probably the most important of all background records and are easily the least understood. National criminal records are *not* available, despite numerous claims by numerous information resellers to the contrary. The FBI has access to the National Crime Information Center (NCIC), but even that has its limitations, as it requires all jurisdictions, even small towns, to submit the information to the index, something that doesn't always happen.

Some states do have statewide databases, which may or may not be available to non-law-enforcement personnel. Some jurisdictions will require record checks by district instead of statewide, and further, sometimes you can only get felonies and not misdemeanors. This could be critical, as frequently these days—with courts bulging at the seams, run by overworked and sometimes incompetent judges—cases are routinely reduced to a misdemeanor from a felony as part of plea negotiations. So a seemingly simple misdemeanor for disorderly conduct may conceal the fact that your subject was originally charged with attempted murder during a bar brawl.

There are any number of public record directories on the market, all of which will spell out availability of criminal records to investigators state by state. Careful research into your state's record accessibility and what you can actually get your hands on is mandatory before telling clients you will provide criminal records.

Employment Verification

Proper employment verification should include not only checking on accuracy of dates but the person's performance, duties performed, eligibility for rehire, and possibly even past salary. This sounds straightforward, but typically the investigator will run into a black hole in the form of the human resources department. HR personnel generally perceive the world in an earthy/crunchy, politically correct perspective that has no resemblance to real life. Somehow, HR personnel find it offensive and counter to nebulous privacy "rights" to provide legitimate information about a person's employment, even if that person has a history of causing mayhem in the office. Mix in corporate attorneys who are litigation-obsessed and you get a roadblock devoid of common sense and reason. These days, going through normal channels may get you dates of employment and not much or nothing else. This is where investigators earn their fees—by being clever, persistent, and devious.

When making an inquiry with an HR rep, listen for clues in the person's tone and inflection that indicate a positive or negative attitude about the subject. Clipped, terse responses imply one thing; rosy asides such as "we were so sorry to see her go" obviously paint a different picture. Be alert to the underlying meaning of buzzwords and phrases, such as "not eligible for rehire" (fired), "met performance standards" (stupid), "laid off due to reorganization" (also fired). Also, try to determine which department the subject worked in and call there, searching for a direct supervisor. Outside of the HR bubble, direct-line supervisors will often tell the truth.

While an application for employment is an official document, falsification of which is grounds for immediate termination, a resume is officially nothing at all and can be as creative as any work of fiction. When reviewing applications and resumes while putting together an employment history, here are some useful tips to follow:

▸ Look not only for gaps in dates of employment but for evidence of filling any gaps in employment, like the Attica convict who said he was running a photography shop. Suspicious gaps usually mean something has been left out, and it is usually for a not-so-nice reason.

▸ Make sure the subject is upwardly mobile. Decreases in salary and/or position generally mean an employment problem or possibly even a termination.

▸ Look for clues in the "Reasons for Leaving" section of the application. Comments such as "personality conflict" might mean the subject is antisocial. "Relocation" must coincide with addresses listed. "Laid off" can mean terminated. Dig deeper for the truth.

▸ Make sure the person's work history fits the job description. People sometimes invent careers and jobs for what they would like to be rather than what they really are. Sort of like the episode in *Seinfeld* where George Constanza claimed he was a marine biologist to impress a woman.

This is a lot more than anyone is ever going to get through human resources at the applicant's previous jobs and is why a trained and doggedly determined investigator is necessary.

Education

No other category on a job application or resume is falsified as much as education. Our experience has been that about 30 percent of all applicants exaggerate their education. People invent entire educational lives, which too often are readily accepted by employers. We've seen multiple degrees materialize out of thin air. No one bothers checking high school diplomas these days, but advanced degrees require scrutiny. Lying about education is, of course, an indication of poor character, but it can also make an unqualified applicant seem qualified, which results in a waste of time and money when it's discovered he's really in over his head.

Unfortunately for people who lie about this part of their lives, education history is usually the easiest to verify. Simply call the college for information; you'll find that the alumni office is usually very forthcoming. One of the unabridged directories of colleges and universities should be a staple in your reference library.

OTHER AREAS OF BACKGROUND CHECKING

Verifying a person's identity and credit, criminal, employment, and education histories is the foundation of a complete background check. However, there are other areas in which a good investigator will dig for pertinent information on an applicant or other subject.

Character References

Employment applications usually request references. The applicant fills in who he or she thinks will give them a good one. These can range from friends and neighbors to cops and senators. Regardless, they are either setups for a good reference, or the applicant is too stupid to list ringers. The PI should call one of these listed references; then, after hearing exactly what was expected, ask, "Who else do you know who knows the subject?" The question catches the reference by surprise, and they often can't think fast enough to provide another ringer, so they give the first name they can think of. The name given is now called a "developed" reference, and a call to that person can often reveal entirely different results and information.

Motor Vehicle Driving Records

This is a must for any applicant who will be driving while on the job, especially if driving a company vehicle. Anyone who has several moving violations should be eliminated from consideration for employment. The company that hires a person with a poor or reckless driving record can be deemed negligent and faced with enormous lawsuits if that employee gets into an accident. It is now possible to get national motor vehicle information online through such sources as Softech International.

Liens and Judgments

Checking civil court records can reveal enormous clues into your subject's character. If he or she has initiated several frivolous lawsuits, there is a good chance the new employer will land on

24

that list of defendants. Conversely, if the subject has been sued several times, that is an obvious red flag. You can check your local courts for this information (it's public record), or a good information reseller such as Lexus/Nexus can provide civil records.

Worker's Compensation Records

You can check worker's comp claims through your state's Department of Labor. This can be very important to a prospective employer, because worker's comp insurance is very expensive—made so by the weight of many claims, often of a suspicious nature. Remember, though, that worker's comp records can only be legally checked *after* the applicant has been offered the job, not before. This protects legitimate claimants from being denied employment unfairly.

HIGH-LEVEL BACKGROUND INVESTIGATIONS

Pre-employment screenings are one thing; they are fiercely fought for by any number of information resellers. What the private eye can get his teeth (or computer) into are the higher-level investigations. An example of this is profiling companies that are a target for acquisition or merger, or ones that are being considered for backing by venture capital firms. This "due diligence" is often done through attorneys, but not always. A PI can solicit venture capital firms directly and generate a nice little business digging up information critical to investors.

This can be highly specialized work, and some of the slicker PIs have come up with inventive ways of gathering information. Analyzing year-end reports and scouring the Web for data are mandatory tasks, but such work could even entail profiling key executives or verifying sales and expenses. A serious effort might include conducting surveillance of the operation and/or putting someone inside undercover. The line to industrial espionage here is thin, however, and a PI must be careful not to step over it.

While pre-employment screening is routinely done on store managers and bank clerks, even companies that should know better will often accept the dazzling resume of a high-ranking executive to be gospel. It can be embarrassing to kick the resume of a prospective top executive over to human resources for verification, so many times companies will outsource this delicate mission to a trusted and respected PI. In such cases, divorce records may be reviewed, assets added up, personal habits researched, and face-to-face interviews conducted. When you think about it, a $1,000 background check on an executive who will be earning in the high six figures is cheap money.

COMPETING WITH INFORMATION RESELLERS

Over the past several years, many companies have streamlined the pre-employment screening process with electronic access to multiple databases. These "information resellers" provide prospective employers with fast and, especially, cheap background checks. Some employers set up terminals in their place of business so the check can be done immediately online. In this way, important records can be researched in a nanosecond. This inexpensive service (often less than $10) is impossible for the struggling PI to compete with—but there is still a niche.

While accessing databases produces a lot of information, it is a little like the federal government attempting to gather intelligence through spy satellites and listening devices with no human intelligence, or HUMINT. Although some of a background screening can be accomplished through a $10 computer check, the real meaty information is acquired on the telephone, or face-to-face if the client has deep pockets. Through conversation, the details and "color" on the subject are learned, which can really provide the depth necessary in the hiring decision. The nuances picked up during a conversation with a human being can make a huge difference in determining future performance, reliability, and integrity. Therefore, the background check done by a competent, insightful PI can be worlds apart from a computer-generated records check. You'll find a certain level of client that prefers this kind of in-depth investigation. Even the large company that obtains a high volume of "production" reports has a need at the upper end of the management pyramid for the more detailed, more subjective reports that a PI can deliver.

The trick to getting this business is to demonstrate the difference to potential clients. Understanding that the PI can never compete with electronic report gathering price-wise, the edge has to be in customer service and analysis of the information gathered. A good PI will develop a rapport with the client to a level where the client comes to rely on the PI's judgment. The investigator can never make the hiring decision, but a "recommendation" can be made for which the client is often very grateful (if a degree of trust has been established). So get into the client's business, meet the decision makers, and get to understand their preferences and personalities. Then provide the information that they really need. This is not to say that obtaining database records is unimportant (it is critically important) or that the computer has replaced the smoking .38 that used to be (in legend) the PI's best friend. But this sort of human intelligence can tip the scales to the higher-priced PI.

REPORTING

The traditional background investigation report was presented in narrative form, arranged by "leads" or areas of investigation, so you had a narrative paragraph under the heading "Identity," another under "Employment History," "Education," and so on. A typical pre-employment background investigation for a middle-level management applicant could fill four or five pages.

Not so anymore. There is a place for detailed narrative reports, and that is for the high-level executive or specialist, where color can be as important as the play-by-play. The computer and, more importantly, our frantic life-style have combined to streamline the basic, production pre-employment report. Programs now frame and template the report, and the investigator simply fills in the blanks with the facts he or she gathers, sometimes while reading questions to the applicant directly from the monitor. These software programs, originally individually written and expensive, are now readily available to all and should be comfortably ensconced in the depths of the PI's trusty computer. While not inexpensive ($1,200 to $2,000 or so), their use can eliminate the need to hire a person for data entry and retrieval and therefore pay for itself in no time.

If a narrative report is called for, the investigator can design it in any way, but he should keep in mind how everyone in business, especially at the decision-making level, is pressed for time.

Reports should be concise, easy to read, and brief. Information critical to the decision should be listed first or highlighted.

Verbal Supplements to Reports

The purpose of the report is to present facts, objectively and unbiased, without recommendations whether or not to hire. But as mentioned earlier, when researching a subject's background, subtle opinions frequently are picked up from interviews. For example, when talking to an employment reference, the only factual information received may be dates of employment and eligibility for rehire. However, the tone of voice and inflection can imply more: possible derogatory feelings and hints that your subject may not be a good candidate for hire.

This is where the PI can prove his worth over the computer-based information reseller. If a good rapport is established with the client and the PI has established credibility, this more subjective "color" can be reported verbally and therefore give much more meaning to the facts, often becoming crucial to the hiring decision. Such subjective thoughts and opinions should not be offered unless this unofficial comfort zone has been established. In fact, it should be avoided completely in a written report to eliminate any threat from liability. Any opinions formed from interviews or other research should be reported very discreetly.

A final word on accuracy. As noted earlier, a background investigation is often called a "consumer report," and strict guidelines have been established to protect the privacy of the applicant and sustain fairness. The most important of these is the Fair Credit Reporting Act, which restricts anyone from researching credit records without proper reason. The 10 permissible purposes cited above must be strictly followed. Also, if employment is declined because of derogatory information contained in the investigator's report, the applicant has the right to know what the information is. If the applicant demands to know why employment was declined, the employer can refer him or her back to the investigative agency that did the report. The agency can protect sources but must provide the report, in total, to the applicant. Any errors or incorrect information must be corrected at the investigative agency's expense. Copies of all reports—narrative or production—should be kept for seven years.

PRICING AND PROFITABILITY

Credit reports are extremely inexpensive for regular users to obtain—$1.50 each for reports online—so the investigator should not try to resell these reports (legally) for high fees. Criminal records costs are all over the board, from practically nothing to $30 or more, depending on the state. Therefore, a credit and criminal combination—a smart report for lower-end personnel—can be priced somewhere around $35. That is an extremely reasonable price for valuable information, especially if the investigator provides some interpretation of the facts.

A standard full report, which would include credit and criminal records, past employments (usually going back five to seven years), education verification, and possibly character references, motor vehicle records, and so forth, can be priced at $85 to $100, depending on the depth of the report. At this rate, the investigator is still operating at a slim profit margin, considering the time and effort involved. However, a regular, ongoing relationship with a client or pool of clients with average report volume can make for a nice occupation.

Even though you may be earning only a couple of bucks per report, you'll find a lot of client resistance to these prices. There are an unbelievably large number of shortsighted employers out there who don't want to pay anything to screen applicants and are always looking for the cheapest possible rate. Never mind that good applicant screening is the cornerstone of any loss-prevention program. Never mind that screening out even one problem employee a year can save the client tens of thousands of dollars. The background investigator is going to have to deal with constant pressure to lower fees.

Better money can be made, but usually with less volume, on the high-end reports. Again, these are the extremely detailed reports on CEOs and other top personnel, which can include anything from newspaper articles and civil judgments to interviews with neighbors. These reports can bring in $200 to $300 each—and occasionally can run as high as $1,000—and are excellent investigative activities.

Likewise, reports on companies—due diligence for venture capital, acquisition, or merger purposes—can command excellent fees, sometimes into the thousands of dollars for extremely detailed reports. Business intelligence is a rapidly growing segment of the PI industry and can be highly lucrative to investigators who specialize in it, but it is a field all to itself, involving profiles of a company's top management and market niche and sometimes complex spreadsheet analyses of sales and growth. Investigators who have the skill set for this work earn top dollar.

The majority of PIs will perform routine background checks and pre-employment screenings. An investigator working alone can expect to complete five to eight standard reports a day. If they are priced somewhere around $85 each, the investigator can gross $500 to $600 per day. Paying for the information online can cost upwards of $25 to $30 per report, giving the PI a net of about $400 a day. Ongoing cases can generate upwards of $1,500 to $2,000 a week. This is still not bad, considering it can all be done in front of a computer, with little or no legwork.

The assignments can come from one large client or several small ones. The trick, as usual, is getting the clients, and getting them to pay reasonable fees. The best and time-tested way to do this is to be professional, understand your clients' needs, and perform to expectations. Customer service is absolutely essential. Even if you are not specializing in these investigations, it's imperative for any professional investigator to know where to find background information, how to interpret it, how to package it, and, most importantly, how to price it.

Ch apter 3
Skip
Tracing

Tracking and finding people—otherwise known as skip tracing—can be a fun part of private investigation and an excellent source of income. Your primary weapons are the telephone, the computer, and your wits, but specialized tools needed for good skip tracing can also be used for a variety of other investigative assignments. So, whether or not you do much of this work, learning to skip trace is an important asset for the private investigator.

Skip tracing, in its finest form, is both a science and an art. The science comes with using available technological tools efficiently. The art comes into play when dealing directly with people. The successful skip tracer has a knack for chatting with possible sources of information and inventing pretexts (legal, of course) to get people to reveal clues to the skip's whereabouts. The investigator learning this aspect of the trade must use initiative, creativity, and cleverness, but experience is the best teacher. Often, hooking up with an experienced and successful tracer is the best way to get an education into finding people, many of whom don't want to be found. Not only can you learn the tricks of the trade this way, but you can hone your creative skills as well.

Besides relying on good investigative skills, the skip tracer absolutely has to know how to use a good electronic crisscross directory and credit report headers. If you are lucky enough to be in a state that allows access to motor vehicle and voter records, you have extra advantages. You can go to www.searchsystems.net

to find thousands of Web sites devoted to accessing public records that will help lead you to the skip.

Credit report headers can give you name verification, possible aliases (or "AKAs," for "also known as"), and at least the last three known addresses. With a previous address, you can go to your cross directory, find a neighbor, and pretext the information you need. Credit headers will also give you Social Security numbers (crucial for further investigation), age or date of birth, and sometimes even a phone number.

Credit headers are available to qualified businesses, including private investigators, through a variety of vendors and information resellers. There are four kinds of credit headers: permissible use headers, GLBA (Gramm-Leach-Bliley Act) headers, non-permissible archive headers, and credit header-based skip tracing databases. This last type is a special product created for skip tracers and provides information from credit headers and other public record databases. Searches can be made by name, address, or Social Security number. Results include current and former addresses, phone numbers, and Social Security numbers. Merlin's Link to America (LTA) is an example of this type of database. Access to credit header-based skip tracing databases is restricted to qualified businesses, including private investigation agencies, that can verify they require the information for appropriate purposes.

An electronic crisscross directory is a national database of names, addresses, and phone numbers that gives you addresses from phone numbers and phone numbers from addresses. If you wanted to talk to a neighbor of a subject, you could simply look up the next house number in the crisscross to get the name and phone number of the person living there, making it easy to call and chat. It is a good investment and will rapidly pay for itself regardless of how much skip tracing you do. The directories are available on CD-ROM, DVD-ROM, and online. While initial costs are about $400, one of these should be in your library.

But don't expect to go to the cross directory and find your subject sitting there. What it gives you more often is the ability to find a phone number for someone who *knows* your subject, or someone who leads you to someone who knows your subject, such as the neighbors at the subject's last address.

Locating these sources with a crisscross database is the science part of skip tracing. The art comes into play when you know how to talk to these people on the phone and get them to give you information without spooking them so much that they tip off the subject.

Being personable, chatty, and polite can mine a wealth of information. You can start by simply asking for help, such as, "Would you be kind enough to help me?" A lot of people are eager to help and, given the opportunity, will bend your ear for as long as you let them about good-old (or that bastard) so-and-so.

If the direct approach doesn't work, you might have to resort to a pretext to trick people into coughing up information. Pretexts are limited only by the deviousness of your imagination. Telling a former neighbor or coworker that you need to reach the subject in order to deliver a package, pay back a loan, summon him for jury duty, or invite him to a class reunion are among the most common. Words to the wise, however: do not use pretexts to try to get banking information, and do not identify yourself as an employee of any real public entities. For example, saying you are with the "Department of Public Safety" would be a no-no; saying you are with the "Department of Security and Safety" could be OK.

REPORTING

As with all investigations, being able to generate a clear, concise, and accurate report is crucial. Even if you can't find the subject—which means no fee—providing a report of the actions you took and leads you followed enhances your credibility and professionalism. If you ran down aliases, searched immigration records, or anything else, even if you weren't successful, detail it all in your report. Conjecture as to the subject's whereabouts is fine, as long as it is defined as such.

PRICING AND PROFITABILITY

Skip tracing is a lucrative talent that can serve as either a primary or additional source of income. Indeed, a good skip tracer can become a much sought-after commodity. Attorneys, banks, collection agencies, bail bondsmen, and others all have need for skip tracing services. Fees can range from $85 to $200 per "hit," and most clients like the "no hit, no fee" concept. It's possible to spend some time and money on an unfindable person, but, with experience and good old-fashioned investigator instincts, the dead-end cases become apparent early on, with a minimum of wasted time and effort.

Ch apter 4
Undercover Investigations

The perception of the undercover investigator in fact and fiction ranges from the true-life grit of Serpico and Donny Brasco to the glamorous fluff of *Charlie's Angels*. The reality of the hardworking PI who provides this service lies somewhere in between.

In the private sector, an undercover investigation—where an investigator goes to work in the client company posing as a regular employee of that company—is the most effective investigative tool available. It can develop and gather information unavailable through any other means. It is like taking an X-ray of the inside operations of a company, detecting issues of employee integrity (good and bad) as well as a wealth of other information crucial to management. Indeed, the undercover investigation may sometimes be the only way to expose and eliminate serious internal problems.

A good undercover investigator ingratiates him or herself into the targeted peer group of the client company and objectively reports on all facets of that operation. It is the HUMINT of investigative work, the "secret agent" of the PI list of services. The work is exceedingly demanding and requires unique investigative skills, and any agent who performs it regularly is subject to burnout. On the other hand, it can be the best entry-level assignment for an investigator in training, as it requires initiative, creativity, objectivity, and sometimes even courage, all essential PI attributes.

THE PRIVATE INVESTIGATOR AS CASE OFFICER

In government intelligence agencies, the case officer recruits, manages, and controls a spy. On a different scale, but similar in many ways, the private investigator running an undercover investigation has to be supervisor, father confessor, coach, and sometimes warden to the undercover investigator. The field agent is "in the cold"—that is, working alone—and needs constant mentoring, support, and guidance. It's ultimately the responsibility of the investigation manager to ensure that the undercover investigator is capable and able to:

- Develop a good cover story and stick to it, yet be able to make appropriate modifications if and when necessary.
- Remember facts without writing them down.
- Ask the right questions of the right people without rousing suspicion.
- Avoid losing objectivity and becoming too close to the subjects of the investigation. Socializing can be the most productive time, but there cannot be actual fraternization or, heaven forbid, any romantic involvement.
- Be a good report writer.
- Understand the laws covering entrapment and not get personally involved in any illegal activity.
- Muster the courage to come out from the cover and give testimony (although this has happened rarely in my 25 years of participating in and supervising undercover work).

SETTING UP THE INVESTIGATION

An undercover investigation is a complex assignment, incorporating the same elements that go into any government- or police-run operation. Let's look at how to get one started.

Insertion

No matter how good an investigator is, nothing happens until he or she is in place and the investigation begins. This takes a bit of collusion between the client and the investigative agency.

It is always best to have the investigator hired into the client company on his own merits rather than being "greased in" by the client. Therefore, it is important that the client provide information so that the investigator can develop a background and story that is "God's gift" to the open position. In order to impress the HR recruiter, the investigator must be tutored on how to respond correctly to questions likely to come up in the interview. Phony references have to be "backstopped" (i.e., ensure they will provide the information you want them to provide), drug and integrity tests have to be passed, and the interview has to go well. Many an assignment has been lost because the investigator couldn't get hired, so the pre-interview preparation has to be thorough.

Protecting the Cover

The cover—the PI's contrived story to justify his or her presence in the company—must be protected at all times, in every way possible. Obviously, this is for a variety of very good reasons, not the least of which is personal safety. Also, even coworkers who are not guilty of misconduct may resent an undercover in their midst, and blowing the cover may compromise the agency's ability to place another undercover investigator in the company in the future.

The cover, therefore, must become an ongoing, living-and-breathing part of the investigator. Ideally, it should be as close to the truth as possible so it is easy to remember and easy to handle slipups. Attention to details is key. The proper clothing, address, even the vehicle being driven can be crucially important to the cover—we've seen cases blown because the investigator failed to remove his college ring when assigned to a warehouse where a high school graduate was hard to find. The investigator must be the square peg in the square hole and fit in by age, race, and demeanor. Even then, penetrating a hard-core clique can be difficult.

Perhaps the biggest danger to the undercover investigator's cover is lack of discretion, i.e., loose lips. We once placed a college graduate as an airport baggage handler. While he was lugging bags, he ran into a guy he went to college with. This young executive, deplaning in his three-piece suit, briefcase in hand, was shocked to see his old classmate in such a low-level job. Our man, to show he was not a failure, whispered his true occupation to his friend, with strict instructions to remain silent about it. Of course, the cover was blown by the end of that business day.

37

In another case, the girlfriend of an undercover investigator was having her hair done in a salon at least 40 miles from the assignment. Keeping with the tradition of telling hairdressers everything, she bragged about the neat job her boyfriend had as a spy in a distribution center. This was on a Saturday. On Monday morning when he arrived for work, three people in the distribution center knew he was a PI.

Creative Cover Development

We were running an undercover investigation in a distribution center, trying to penetrate a theft and drug ring. Although the investigator fit in with the targeted group in every way, they were suspicious of anyone relatively new and, while not suspecting him, kept him at arm's length. It was summer, and most of the subjects of the investigation would sit outside on picnic tables during their lunch break, essentially ostracizing our guy, who, no matter how hard he tried, ended up pretty much alone.

So, one nice hot day, while our investigator sat a short distance away from the group, we rolled in a large, black Cadillac, driven by a large, bad-looking black guy. In the passenger seat we placed an attractive blonde sporting a white blouse (opened low enough to be interesting), large earrings, and a foxy look. The driver pulled up next to our man, reached out the car window, and gave him a wad of cash. They quickly bumped fists; then the Cadillac and its heart-stopping passenger drove away at a high speed and the investigator went back to his sandwich without a word. Shortly thereafter, he became very popular with the bad guys and was brought into the group. They now assumed he was an impressive criminal and couldn't wait to bring him in on their scams and illegal activities.

MANAGING THE CASE

Once hired, the investigator has to learn his new job and get to know his new coworkers. Therefore, it is always best to start slow, not asking questions that are in any way suspicious and doing whatever is necessary to not get fired. Being on the job long enough to become one of the group is of paramount importance. If and when this is accomplished, the rest of the case usually flows easily.

The investigator should, as much as possible, come to work early and leave late. These are the times when bad things often happen. Seemingly insignificant details such as where cars are parked, who is spending money, and who is doing who can be critically important to develop leads. The investigator cannot be squeaky clean, nor can he be a ringleader of dishonest employees. He's got to be somewhere in the middle. Remember, all rules of entrapment—that is, tempting or coercing someone to do a criminal act that they would not otherwise have the propensity to do—must be clearly understood at the onset and followed to the letter. For example, asking, "Do you know where I can buy drugs?" is not entrapping someone if they respond positively. But you cannot say, "Help me buy some drugs and I'll give you money" (or sex or whatever). That is entrapment.

If the investigator uncovers drug use, he cannot ingest controlled substances, even if other employees are doing so and urge him to join in. There are clever ways to simulate ingestion or make denials for health or other reasons. Ingesting a controlled substance is a criminal act and can compromise the investigation.

If a drug buy is deemed important, the proper way to go about it is to notify local law-enforcement authorities about the case on an official level, discuss the anticipated purchase, and make arrangements to turn over any purchased suspected drugs. This is important to protect the investigator from arrest for possession. (If you think you're going to get any such deal in writing, forget it. These are unofficial understandings.) Lab analysis is necessary to determine exactly what kind of drugs are being sold, and this is always best done through law-enforcement laboratories. Strict chain-of-custody rules must be followed.

The undercover investigator is constantly buried with an enormous amount of information. Consider all the things that happen to a person during a routine, mundane day; then consider all that an investigator has to remember and sort out as to which is important or not to the case. Facts have to be prioritized and remembered accurately. It is always best to report actual quotes from the subjects of the investigation. Writing things down during the workday cannot be done; it's too dangerous, too suspicious, and guaranteed to blow the cover. Dictating into a tape recorder at the end of the shift works sometimes; we've had investigators hide a recorder in their car and tape their notes when safely away from the premises. But again, he or she has to be especially careful not to be seen or allow the tape recorder to be discovered. However it is worked out, the investigator must make clear notes *that day* to keep the information fresh and meaningful.

Daily reports should be condensed into a weekly report, which is submitted immediately to the case manager. The manager must make sure the standard "who, what, when, where, why, and how" are answered and that the report is complete. Analysis of the information is also the responsibility of the case manager; the undercover investigator cannot be required to interpret on top of gathering accurate, objective information.

As much information as possible should be delivered. More is never too much. It need not be limited to serious instances of dishonesty, substance abuse, or other criminal activity. Information on morale, supervision, loitering, efficiency, and even gossip can be of crucial importance to the client. The following is a list of the areas that can be targeted and reported on during a typical undercover investigation:

- Financial dishonesty
    Theft of cash or merchandise
    Price alteration
    Fraudulent returns
    Unauthorized discounts
    Kickbacks
    Unreported shortage in merchandise from vendors
    Padded expenditures

- Narcotics
    Sale, either on the clock and/or on the premises
    Ingestion, either on the clock and/or on the premises

- Supervision
    Lack thereof
    Sexual harassment
    Poor judgment
    Favoritism

Lack of employees' respect
Poor scheduling
Unnecessary overtime
Poor training
Poor recordkeeping
Poor stocking, housekeeping, or maintenance

- Work performance
  Falsification of time records
  Falsification of production records
  Idling—deliberate, or from lack of work
  Gambling
  Drinking
  Unauthorized or overstaying reliefs
  Arguing or fighting
  Misuse of company materials
  Careless handling of merchandise
  Leaving early
  Absenteeism
  Tardiness
  Profanity, obscenity
  Sexual harassment
  Failure to cooperate
  Smoking
  Unauthorized phone calls
  Rowdiness
  Eating in department

- Security
  Guard activities
  Exit security
  Employee identification
  Key control
  Lock-up practices
  Fences and enclosures
  Alarms and time clocks
  Security at shipping and receiving docks
  Cashier's office security
  Cash register security

Sealing or locking of vehicles
Computer or database access
Pass system for removal of merchandise
Persons in unauthorized areas
Fire safety and prevention
Storage of materials
Night security
Sabotage to equipment or merchandise
Workplace violence awareness

- Employer/employee relations
    Attitudes
    Turnover
    Promotions
    Overtime
    Suggestion system
    Rumors
    Bonus and pay scales
    Facilities and benefits

- Systems and procedures
    Cash flow channels
    Information sharing
    Communication issues between departments
    Communication issues between management and staff

- Personnel evaluations
    Work habits
    Honesty
    Character, integrity
    Morals
    Courtesy
    Abilities
    Background
    Ambitions
    Potential

Investigator Guidelines
While undercover investigators are often nonconformists,

leading toward renegade, and operate (by necessity) on their own, it is important that they operate within structured guidelines. The following is a list of policies and procedures that must be followed throughout the assignment:

- Reports must never be falsified or unsubstantiated. Falsification of a report is grounds for immediate dismissal. Information should always be objective; if information is subjective or an opinion, it must be identified as such.
- All reports must be timely.
- Specific results of investigations must never be revealed to outside parties.
- No information should be given to a client without authorization from a supervisor.
- Firearms or weapons of any kind must be approved in writing by the case manager before being carried on assignment. (It's not a bad idea to get approval from the client as well, although this does not happen all the time.)
- Do not become overly friendly or fraternize with the client's employees outside of the assignment.
- Never admit to being an investigator.
- Never take risks.
- Never borrow or lend money or take gifts from clients or their employees.
- Never refer friends to a client for a job.
- Never get involved romantically with any of the client's personnel.
- Maintain daily contact with the case manager.

Finding individuals with the character and integrity to adhere to these guidelines at all times can be tricky, but it can be done. Look for candidates among criminal justice majors in local colleges, store detectives, or even security guards who are a cut above average and want to develop a career. Undercover experience in the private sector counts a lot for background experience if the person is pursuing a career in law enforcement, especially with agencies like the FBI, so anyone who is entering the criminal justice field is usually a good candidate for a first undercover assignment with a private investigation agency.

ENDING THE CASE WITH THE COVER INTACT

An undercover investigator must protect his identity throughout the investigation to safeguard his best interests as well as the interests of the client. Again, employees may resent the client for placing a private investigator on staff, even if they are guilty of no misconduct, and anyone fingered for misconduct by the PI obviously will not be happy with him. Therefore, an undercover PI should preserve his cover to the end. This can go as far as working out an arrangement with the client and the police to be "busted" along with other employees as a result of the investigation, assuming the case is going to end at the time an arrest or apprehension is made. This will convince the other arrestees that the undercover is "one of them" and divert suspicion. Should the undercover ever be confronted and accused of being a "spy" or "narc," he or she should remain cool and simply follow the old rule—deny, deny, deny—then demand proof and make counter allegations.

PITFALLS AND PLUSES OF UNDERCOVER WORK

While there are a lot of good things about the undercover investigations business, nothing is really easy. First of all, finding good people for this line of work is tough. A career undercover investigator is a rare bird indeed. Living two lives is stressful (again, think Serpico and Brasco) and requires a special commitment. Most investigators will do one or two assignments, then ask to move on.

But there is an upside. We've found that hiring and training the right person for an undercover assignment is an excellent entry-level path into the field, providing you give the new investigator the support needed. In fact, if you find a good undercover, that individual will most likely be good at all types of investigations, mainly because an undercover has to possess all of the basic traits necessary to PI work, including the ability to think on one's feet, sharp powers of observation, good people skills, keen memory, and a talent for report writing. Most of the senior staff in my agency started as undercover investigators.

Another major negative to undercover work is that each assignment, by its very nature, is goal orientated. Whether it lasts six weeks or six months, it has an end. (Although we've had one client who has had an undercover investigator inside—not the same one—for almost 20 years. He says he is able to sleep at night knowing that he knows everything that is going on.) Therefore, you have to continuously find clients with a need and desire (and budget) for an internal investigation.

Once established, and with successfully completed cases under your belt, you'll find that clients will come back to you periodically for more assignments, but you can't hold your breath. While it is possible to solicit new companies for these jobs, you have to maintain the discretion associated with the covert nature of the work, and you usually have to get to top people. Don't think a human resource manager will request an assignment.

On the other hand, if you get in the right doors, you'll find that a wide variety of industries will realize that they have the need. Hospitality services will use undercover waitresses, bartenders, and kitchen help to ferret out theft and drug use. Distribution and manufacturing will frequently use investigators on the shipping/receiving dock and other vulnerable locations. Hospitals control such things as drug theft and patient abuse with undercover people. Even movie theaters, being a mostly cash business, have a significant need. The trick is to convince the right people at the right time of the positive impact of an undercover investigation. Properly run, there will never be an internal investigation that will disappoint your client. And generally, the success of an undercover investigation will raise your stock significantly in the client's eye and make it much easier to discuss other jobs (surveillance, background checks, etc.).

Another role for undercover investigators, whispered about but seldom discussed openly, is their offensive use in unsuspecting companies. Unethical (not to mention illegal) agencies may insert people in companies at the behest of competitors to conduct industrial espionage, acquire company secrets, or even steal proprietary information for personal gain. On the flip side, some companies use undercover people to determine if they have been penetrated by rival companies (or even countries) looking to steal information.

There are, at times, legitimate reasons to insert a "plant" in an unsuspecting company, such as to target illegal activities and gather evidence. But these times are rare and risky. Laws against industrial espionage have been tightened recently, with convictions resulting in enormous fines and sometimes even prison time. Penetrating unsuspecting entities should be left to the CIA and other world-class spy agencies. Done properly, it takes considerable preparation, large monetary investment, and a unique, motivated, and competent investigator. While the PI can demand giant fees for this activity, it is not recommended.

REPORTING

Information gathered during an undercover investigation is worthless without fast and accurate dissemination. While information contained in the reports is what the client is paying for, the quality of the investigative process is reflected in the reports. Consequently, complete, well-written reports must be a top priority.

During the course of any undercover investigation, there may well be days when seemingly nothing of interest happens. This is never the case! During any day, many things occur, good and bad. Even if public enemy number one is not discovered on a particular day, some people work hard, some don't; rumors fly; supervision is good or sloppy; security and other procedures are followed or ignored. All of this type of information can make excellent content for a report. Remember that an undercover investigation uncovers information that is unavailable through any other means. Even if nothing bad is detected, a report can still give the client a clear idea of how his operation is running, who is a good or bad employee, and what he needs to change to improve things. Even seemingly unimportant information gathered during the investigation can be crucial to the client. There can never be too much information, unless the client specifically requests streamlined reports (covered below).

Do's and Don'ts of Undercover Investigation Reporting

Do:
- Answer who, what, when, where, why, and how for each situation.
- Be extremely timely.

46

- Report on the positive as well as the derogatory.
- Be objective.
- Clearly identify all persons reported.

Don't:
- Entrap.
- Report on lawful union activities.
- Be subjective, unless clearly identified as such.
- Assume without cause.

The undercover investigator will best remember the sequence of events and will generally provide the most information by preparing chronological daily reports. Weekly and final reports also can be organized chronologically, or they can be categorized by topic, recording observations on such areas as employee dishonesty, substance abuse, supervision quality, and so on. We've found that the most popular form of report gives a summary of important items by topic at the beginning, then goes through the details in chronological sequence.

PRICING AND PROFITABILITY

Undercover investigations can be very profitable in that the client, while employing the investigator, pays part of his or her salary. Therefore, payroll costs for you are relatively low. For example, a quality undercover investigator will be worth $20 or more an hour. However, the client will pay the field agent as a regular employee, which may be anywhere from $8 to $15 an hour (for a warehouse or similar low-level position). You only have to pay the difference.

Your fee also includes management of the case, advice and consultation, and clerical costs, but an undercover investigation can, and should, generate collateral fees for additional services. Practically every case can result in the need for interviews and interrogations, surveillances and/or hidden cameras to monitor suspicious activity, and background checks on suspected bad guys. In fact, some agencies look at undercover assignments as valuable profit vehicles, garnering greater fees from the extra services required.

Charging for an undercover investigation will be determined

partly by the position being filled (e.g., dock worker or management trainee), the industry (retail, hospitality, manufacturing, etc.), and the quality and experience of the investigator. For assignments in manufacturing or distribution, an average undercover rate would come in at between $700 and $900 per 40-hour week. You may be paying your investigator $20 to $25 per hour, but $10 of that will come from your client. Therefore, a 40-hour week will cost you about $400 to $600 in payroll; the balance is gross profit.

In more high-tech firms such as financial institutions, medical centers, and computer companies, it is not unusual to charge $1,200 or more a week. I've seen some agencies charge flat rates of $5,000 per month. These are usually for tried and proven investigators, but even so, considering that undercover assignments will usually last two to three months, it can be a real profit maker.

Some industries, such as large retailers that have established loss-prevention departments and experienced directors, will ask for lower fees in exchange for abbreviated reports. Sometimes the reports can simply be check-off sheets if the director is targeting specific people or locations for known problems. This is fine, as long as you can still maintain an acceptable profit margin working at the discounted rate. We give discounts if the client wants multiple investigators at the same time, and we offer a 20 percent discount to favored clients. About 50 percent of total fees taken in should fall to the bottom line, an amount even the most inefficient agency can live with.

Chapter 5
Insurance Investigations

There is work to be had in insurance investigations, usually pretty hard work, and agencies involved in it generally specialize in it. This is for very good and simple reasons, the most important being the relationship the agency needs to develop with the client, the insurance company.

Fraudulent insurance claims are first examined by the company's claims adjuster and then may be kicked over to its special investigations unit (SIU). Into this mix the private investigator is sometimes stirred. The insurance carrier may have excess claims it has to outsource. It may not have a viable SIU, or it may determine that it's simply cheaper to farm out the questionable claims to an outside investigator. In every instance, the PI gets assigned cases through contacts and relationships with managers, claims adjusters, SIU directors, or other decision makers in the insurance company.

The majority of the investigative action is directed against worker's compensation fraud, or "worker's comp" cases, where the insurance company suspects the claimant is faking an injury to collect compensation. There are also property loss fraud and arson investigations. All these cases tend to be labor intensive, although the most successful investigators use guile, ingenuity, and cleverness to unravel them.

WORKER'S COMP CASES

If an employee claims that an injury is preventing him from working, and fraud is suspected by the insurance company, the PI has to prove that the employee is really able to perform physical activity and is not suffering as claimed. These cases typically call for "activity checks" on the subject. Usually an insurance company will authorize a small budget for this work, generally only covering a couple hours of surveillance to see if the case seems worth pursuing. But the investigator has to be lucky as well as good with such limited time and resources. There are infinite ways to defraud an insurance company for benefits, and infinite ways to cover it up, making the life of the investigator miserable. Straight surveillances for a couple of hours are a crapshoot, and the PI will probably have to be creative and even use some unpaid time to develop the case.

The classic investigator for these assignments was the nondescript guy with the zoom lens on his camera, staking out the subject. Peeking over the fence and photographing the claimant performing physical activity still is a common way to solve these cases and, in fact, the majority of this work consists of long, boring surveillance. However, the PI has to be cognizant and respectful of trespass laws and privacy issues. Solid cases have been thrown out (and sometimes charges brought against the PI) because of trespass accusations. And a "reasonable expectation of privacy" (yes, that is a legal designation based on the Fourth Amendment of the U.S. Constitution) extends to the inside of a home as well as backyards and adjacent areas.

There are other problems with surveillance stakeouts. Workman comp cases frequently require surveillance in residential neighborhoods, subjecting the investigator to nosy neighbors, roving dogs, curious kids, and neighborhood watches. Cops are called about the suspicious stranger all too often, blowing the surveillance or at least embarrassing the investigator. Therefore, it is almost always better to call the police and inform them of the surveillance ahead of time, giving them a description of you and your vehicle. Because of the risk of the police somehow tipping off your target, a little disinformation may be necessary, such as telling them you are in the neighborhood on a divorce case. Some police believe that that's all PIs do, so that reason makes perfect sense to them.

If there are concerns about trespass, privacy, or undisturbed access to the claimant, another way to solve a fraudulent worker's comp case is to approach the claimant directly and get him to admit to it. This is not possible if he is represented by counsel, but if not, sometimes he can tell you exactly what you want to know. A time-tested ploy is to send an attractive young woman to the subject's house posing as a market research surveyor. Armed with a bag of "free samples" of the product being discussed (toothpaste, for example), she asks for a few minutes of his time to answer questions for market research purposes. After the series of dumb questions about the product, the researcher gets around to "demographic" information and works in questions about employment. Done correctly, the subject often brags about the extra jobs he has secretly on the side. There are many variations of this kind of pretext questioning, but again, the investigator has to be careful about infringing on rights, particularly if the subject is represented by an attorney.

Here's another example of using cleverness and creativity to yield results. I once took on a case to prove the subject was not completely disabled as he claimed. It turned out that he lived on a narrow country road, making it impossible to set up a surveillance post. Further, the house was set way back and was guarded by a couple of large, unfriendly dogs. However, a walk in the woods behind the house revealed an enormous pile of firewood and log-splitting equipment. A clue!

A scenario was set up where a bogus real estate agent (again, an attractive young woman) went to the house and inquired about land for sale. Noticing the pile of wood in back, she innocently asked the subject if he sold the wood. When he eagerly answered affirmatively, she asked to buy some. But alas, the sports car she was driving was unsuitable for log hauling. She could, however, borrow her brother's truck and meet the subject at a shopping center nearby. Our man, eager to impress the young lady and make some money, agreed. Of course, I was set up with camera in hand in the back of the lot, getting some juicy incriminating shots of the subject picking up large logs, carrying them around, and even throwing them into the truck. Insurance claim denied.

OTHER INSURANCE ASSIGNMENTS

Although worker's comp investigations pretty much consist of drudgework, some insurance work is high level and can yield high-level fees. Exposing fraudulent claims of property loss is one example. Often, insurance companies will pay a percentage of recoveries, and some property loss cases can be enormous. You old guys will remember the TV series *Banacek* that followed the exploits of a fictional insurance investigator who raked in serious cash for solving tough-to-crack cases.

Another area of specialization in the insurance field is arson investigations. Arson investigators must respond quickly to a scene and gather evidence for laboratory analysis before it becomes tainted. Armed with a case of Mason jars to gather chunks of burned debris for evidence, the arson investigator fills a unique and vital niche for insurance companies. Of course, he has to be qualified—the work requires a level of technical training to determine, among other things, if accelerants have been used for an intentional burn—and he has to be ready to go 24/7.

This specialized service generally commands higher fees, but the PI who does it is exposed to swings in the economy. When things are good, fewer bad guys burn down their restaurants and buildings; when things are bad, the arson investigator thrives. Also, improvements in modern construction and the widespread use of fire and smoke detectors has resulted in smaller and less catastrophic fires, reducing the need for private arson investigators. These days, most are retired fire chiefs or firefighters, but opportunities still do exist for anyone willing to learn the technicalities of the work.

REPORTING

Insurance investigation reports are generally narrative; however, insurance companies cannot live without their special headings and codes. The lone wolf investigator has got to remember that insurance companies are bureaucracies in the classic sense of the word, and reports will find themselves on several desks before any kind of decision is made, including authorization for payment to the investigator.

Therefore, make sure all reports start with the proper industry heading, which will list the case reference number and other internal information. Following that, reports have got to be brief and efficient, with little or no subjective information. Photos and videos are crucial—any report lacking those will not be taken as seriously, regardless of its content—but insurance companies are much more comfortable when the report provides written details that indicate the investigator was conscientious and diligent. Descriptions of residences, vehicles, and even the neighborhood will lend credence to the report, so don't fall into the trap of thinking that photo and video evidence alone—damning as it may be—will suffice.

PRICING AND PROFITABILITY

Insurance companies generally prefer to raise premiums across the board rather than spend money to eliminate fraudulent claims. In other words, it's much easier to simply pay the claim, regardless of how bogus it looks, and screw the policyholders with higher premiums. Therefore, most insurance companies spend their investigative dollars fairly gingerly. This is especially true if they have an in-house SIU.

The budget for a typical activity report on a worker's comp case will probably be under $400, or less than eight hours of surveillance. Considering your subject may be working or playing part time; mornings, days, or nights; or weekdays or weekends, you know you have to be lucky as well as good to crack a case that fast. Sometimes it takes a couple of hours just to set up the surveillance post, and sometimes the surveillance is blown by unforeseen events. With such short billing, worker's comp work requires volume; the more cases and hours, the better bottom line. If you're going to specialize in this area, investment in a well-equipped surveillance van can make all the difference in the world. The initial outlay for video and camera gear, mini fridge or coolers, cot, portable waste disposal system (i.e., bathroom), and customization work to the van will be large, but it is essential if you're going to be successful at lengthy surveillances.

Again, arson work demands higher fees because of the specialized expertise required, and the fact that there are not so many experienced investigators around also keeps fees high. Billing around $100 an hour is not unheard of for a seasoned arson investigator.

Property loss cases can be done on an hourly basis or on a percentage of the recovery or savings to the insurance company. There can be real money in this, as these cases tend to be very large—after all, it's stupid to try to defraud an insurance company for chump change, and the companies do not assign PIs to look into small claims. Declining the claim or recovering the losses in fraudulent cases can have a significant impact on an insurance company's bottom line, and getting a 20 to 30 percent cut of that impact can be very lucrative to the private investigator.

Ch apter 6
Attorney Work

Every successful investigator or agency has some attorney clients. Some have only attorney clients. Some have only one attorney client. There is a broad range of investigative work needed by a broad range of attorneys. Let's look at some of them:

- Personal injury attorneys need information about the scene of the incident and the history of the defendant.
- Divorce and custody attorneys need the dirt on spouses and ex-spouses that investigators can give them.
- Product liability attorneys need scene investigations and court histories.
- Corporate attorneys need due diligence, background, and financial information.
- Intellectual property attorneys need information from the field on trademark infringements.
- Criminal attorneys require all sorts of information.

The list goes on and on. The point is that all of the above assignments call for the types of skills that any decent PI should possess. Scene investigation for an accident, for example, requires measuring distances, researching weather reports, finding witnesses, and taking as many photos as possible. (The various *CSI* television series are really very good in depicting the kind of critical attention to detail that goes into scene investigations.) A divorce case could entail a background check, surveillance, and even pretexting to get the goods on the target spouse. You get the picture.

FINDING WORK

In every community, there is usually a legal newspaper or newsletter that serves the legal community. In Boston, it's *Lawyer's Weekly*. The top publication in your community can easily be found on the Internet. These periodicals are great outlets in which to advertise your services and get introduced to firms and individual attorneys. One-time ads generally do little for name recognition, so the PI has to be prepared to place an eye-catching ad and run it many times in a row. Emphasis on your verifiable experience and credentials is key, and it's a good idea to state that you specialize in investigations for the legal profession.

Once one or two attorneys seek assistance, the PI will become more and more known in the local legal community, building business over time. Attorneys are like everyone else—they have little time to shop around. When they need something, they go to who they know, who they have heard of, or who has been recommended to them. Name recognition is everything.

Dropping in to large firms and leaving brochures and business cards can generate work, as long as you always remember that lawyers bill by time, and to interrupt them and take their time can be self-defeating. Looking sharp, smiling, and projecting a competent, professional demeanor as you leave brochures and business cards with the receptionist will make a good first impression and usually get your information in front of someone, increasing your odds of picking up cases. Better yet, try to identify and arrange an appointment with the administrative head of the office.

Once on board, you'll find that lawyers, believe it or not, are somewhat loyal, and the work can become steady. Some large law firms retain the ongoing services of several investigators for individual members of the firm. Other larger firms might need outside investigative assistance infrequently, and they often kick over research work to their paralegals, so there may be long droughts between assignments.

Lawyers like an investigator who seems to specialize in their field. While the PI can "specialize" in a lot of fields, it is good to give the impression that the client's field (say, intellectual property) is your forte. Background research is absolutely necessary for virtually all attorney work, so excellent computer skills are mandatory. Be aware that paralegals and lawyer's assistants are often highly skilled in Internet research, so the PI has to be at least equal, if not more competent, in digging out useful information online to make an impression.

REPORTING

Attorneys have their own language and tend to correspond in that legalese. Therefore, it is important to have a "RE" line (for "regarding") in the heading of every letter and report, which should include the name of the subject (plaintiff or defendant) and file number, if available.

Attorneys generally have a nanosecond of concentration, so reports should be brief, containing all the facts in a summarized (or bullet point) format. If it is a short report, put it in letter form, as attorneys are accustomed to letters. Don't be offended if your information is never acted on or ends up playing a bit part in a bigger case. An attorney preparing for a case will generally seek all kinds of information and sort it out as needed. So be brief, but don't leave anything out or self-edit your findings.

PRICING AND PROFITABILITY

Some investigators who do only attorney work make a nice living out of it. These usually are PIs who have hooked up with a high-powered lawyer who has a full calendar and needs a good investigator to augment almost every case. Often the relationship becomes very close and is long term—one hand washes the other, and the success of one hinges on the other. A PI who gets into this kind of comfortable association can do very well, especially if the lawyer is doing very well. Even Perry Mason had his sidekick PI.

Fees range all over the place, from $45 an hour for individual (usually personal injury) attorneys to $200 an hour for large, prestigious firms. However, getting the big fees will require becoming a preferred (and often exclusive) investigator engaged in large litigation cases.

One of the problems with attorney work, and it can be a big problem, is that it's often hard—sometimes impossible—to get paid. Lawyers are really good at sending bills and usually really bad at paying them. Work against a retainer if possible. That, however, may be tough, as an attorney will usually pass on as much billing as possible to the client, investigative services included. In other words, you don't get paid until the attorney does, and never before.

Ch apter 7
Intellectual Property Investigations

An area of specialization that's largely unknown and often ignored is the investigation and control of trademark infringements, or IP (for intellectual property) investigations. Companies, particularly manufacturers and sellers of high-end merchandise, spend millions of dollars to develop a trademark name and/or logo. These trade names are very familiar to all—in the area of luxury apparel and accessories, think Rolex, Coach, Louis Vuitton, and Chanel.

Just as familiar to everyone are "knockoffs," or counterfeit imitations of these products. Walk down the busy retail sections of big cities like New York and Los Angeles and you'll find sidewalk vendors brazenly selling all sorts of counterfeit merchandise. The interesting thing about knockoffs is that most people look at them as simple bargains and not as something that is in the least bit wrong, let alone illegal.

Fact of the matter is that the manufacture and distribution of counterfeit merchandise cost the trademark holders millions in lost revenue, and it can injure or even destroy brand names that have taken years to develop. In some cases—such as medicines, or automobile and aircraft parts—imitations, almost always inferior to the branded originals, can create dangerous malfunctions that can lead to injuries and death. Of course, most counterfeit merchandise is of retail products, which, while not causing accidents, can certainly hurt the bottom line of the original company.

Intellectual property crime is an enormous international problem that is extremely difficult, if not impossible, to combat. Such countries as China and Russia turn a blind eye to counterfeiting, and it is rampant there, but it takes place in other regions as well. There is rumor of a state-sponsored factory in Croatia making fake Chanel perfume. Software companies such as Microsoft are victimized throughout the world, with versions of their products turning up in other languages almost immediately after being released on the market. The film and recording industries suffer greatly from counterfeit DVDs and CDs sold around the world. (People will actually go into a theater for a popular first-run movie, videotape it with a camcorder, and produce thousands of knockoff DVDs.) Even terrorist organizations have been known to make and sell counterfeit products to finance their murderous activities.

Law enforcement has little or no inclination to attack trademark infringement because of more pressing matters elsewhere. Yet the problem has grown so huge that some companies have created entire divisions to try to combat it. Assisting companies in the control of this fraudulent activity can be very lucrative for the right agency or investigator. If you're in the right market and can get established, this can be an extraordinarily lucrative gig, and is nice, clean work to boot.

ESTABLISHING YOURSELF

To be a player in this field, you've got to play with the big boys. Trademark infringement is important to the top-tier companies of branded merchandise. Not many people are going to counterfeit JC Penny merchandise, so you've got to be comfortable swimming in the pool with executives from the likes of Versace, Louis Vuitton, Calvin Klein, Rolex, and others at that luxury level. These are people who earn big money, run at the highest echelons of our culture, and demand results. Getting to the right people can be tough, but if and when it's done once, it can be the start of a beautiful relationship.

The control of intellectual property is changing rapidly with the advent of all kinds of electronic and other monitoring systems. These range from identifying chips (including GPS) being secreted into the product to special inks, nonduplicating logos, and other high-tech means of attacking this global problem. The investigator must be aware of these innovations, be prepared to work with them, and use traditional investigative skills to augment them. Like everything else, high-tech controls will never completely replace a good field investigator.

A lot of counterfeit merchandise is very good and can be difficult for the layman to discern from the real thing. In fact, it's often difficult for experts to discern the difference. Therefore, everything begins with establishing whether or not the merchandise is indeed counterfeit.

GETTING A CASE

Most cases are initiated when the investigator comes upon suspicious merchandise at flea markets, on push carts along busy city streets, or in retail stores. The Internet is also a source for counterfeit merchandise. Some investigators have generated income by surfing the Net, finding questionable merchandise for sale, and following up with a viable case.

Another common place where counterfeit merchandise is sold is in private "house parties," such as the classic Tupperware or lingerie parties. The bad guys can control their exposure with private parties, as only invited guests can be there and, of course, private detectives and cops are rarely on the guest list. These are classic targets for undercover investigators, almost all of whom will be female. We've actually initiated our own parties where, unknown to the bad guys, *all* of the guests were investigators.

Obviously, the amount of merchandise and the size of the crooked dealer will determine the size of the case. Most trademark holder companies are interested in what are called "piece counts" of the amount of counterfeit merchandise recovered or destroyed and will pay according to the size of the seizure or illegal operation.

Let's take an example of a small boutique store in an out of the way place selling, say, Coach handbags. The alert PI spots the suspicious merchandise being sold. Establishing a proper cover (anything from a typical customer to a dealer him or herself), the investigator eyeballs the place and tries to get an accurate piece count of the items being sold. Then a "controlled buy" has to be made (at the investigator's expense). A controlled buy is nothing more than a purchase of the suspected merchandise that documents all of the facts surrounding the purchase, such as model name or number, price, location of purchase, time and date of purchase, and so on. Then a normal chain of custody has to be followed.

The investigator has now purchased a couple of pieces of suspected counterfeit merchandise, has a thorough report of the purchases, and has the suspect merchandise in his possession. Now here's the hard part: the PI has to contact the right person at the trademark holder company—usually an attorney or one of the in-house finance people—and explain the circumstances. In this example, the investigator contacts a staff attorney representing Coach and provides the facts to date. If the company is interested, the attorney will ask for a proposal as to cost and methodology for dealing with the store. The PI will then be told to send the suspect merchandise to the company for analysis in order to determine if it is truly counterfeit.

Often, more than one brand of knockoff item is being sold at a location. This can be a big plus to the PI because now the cost of the investigation can be split between two or more companies, making them more willing to assign the case because their expenses are less. So, if the investigator spots Louis Vuitton and Coach in the same place, the investigation will be outlined, then approximate costs developed and divided between the two trademark holders. The split is determined by the quantity of the counterfeit merchandise in each brand. For example, if there are 50 Louis Vuitton handbags and only 25 Coach handbags, Louis Vuitton would shoulder twice the cost of the investigation as Coach.

CLOSING A CASE

There are several ways to deal with sellers and/or manufacturers of counterfeit merchandise.

Cease and Desist
The first is a cease and desist demand and voluntary surrender of the merchandise. In this scenario, the PI

hand-delivers a letter (usually drafted by company attorneys) to the bad guy demanding he "cease and desist" from selling the merchandise. Generally, civil and/or criminal actions are threatened if the cease and desist order is ignored. The investigator also asks the bad guy to surrender the merchandise. This "surrender" is voluntary, and the seller of the merchandise can refuse. However, if the PI has a command presence and is professional, it's amazing how many people will turn over the goods. A forceful demand will often result in the investigator driving away with a car full of merchandise.

The trademark holder will generally tell the investigator to destroy the merchandise. This can be done by turning it into a dump and getting a receipt. While trademark holders seldom follow up to see if the counterfeit products have been destroyed, it does not make sense for the investigator to cheat and let the stuff flow back into the marketplace. The damage to the PI's credibility would be devastating if it ever were to be discovered.

Further Investigation

Another way to deal with the situation is to call for further investigation into the origin of the merchandise. This authorization does not happen frequently, but it can in cases of large quantities being brought into the country or manufactured in clandestine plants. This can be a large and lucrative case for the PI. Some investigations have lasted years and can involve organized crime or even terrorist groups. The work is generally traditional in nature, usually surveillance and/or undercover work. If the mails are being used, records from the U.S. Postal Service and other shipping companies are retained to gauge the quantity and track the flow of the merchandise.

In a large or extended investigation, law enforcement such as the FBI or U.S. Customs usually get involved and work with the investigator. Sometimes the PI is muscled out of a case by the feds, but more often he will remain on the case to protect the interests of his client, the trademark holder. The investigator may not lead the investigation, but he will still be involved and cooperate with the authorities.

In his role as representative of the client, the PI should be sure to:

- Identify and certify that the merchandise being confiscated is indeed counterfeit.
- Count and tag the confiscated merchandise for the trademark holder's information.
- Arrange for safe storage of the merchandise, the cost of which is usually borne by the trademark holder.

How does the PI accomplish these tasks without butting heads with the law-enforcement agents in charge of the case? Basically, by not being an asshole. The relationship between law enforcement and private investigators is an interesting topic. Police and federal agents generally consider private investigators to be a necessary evil. The investigator has to be sensitive to the dynamics of law-enforcement personnel and be very cooperative and supportive of their efforts. Once the PI's credibility is established, working with law enforcement becomes easy, as the officers will realize the PI can do things they cannot.

Raid and Arrest

In this scenario, generally done when there is a fairly large quantity of merchandise to recover, the investigator will initiate law enforcement's involvement (with the consent of the client) and provide enough information to have probable cause to obtain a search warrant. Then, local law enforcement or a federal outfit like Customs or the FBI will raid the premises, confiscate all the counterfeit merchandise, and charge the bad guy with criminal complaints relating to the operation.

We did a case where enterprising bad guys got ahold of a large quantity of counterfeit apparel and were selling bits and pieces through a small retail store. I posed as a guy from a flea market out of state and asked if I could buy in quantity. After some Hollywood acting, I got invited out to a warehouse, where they had about 20,000 pieces. I was (in my role) very excited and asked if I could buy the whole quantity. After a bit of negotiation we worked out an agreement, and I was told to come back with my helpers and truck to take possession of the goods. Getting the trademark holder on board and coordinating with the FBI, I came back a couple of days later with my rental truck and four helpers. After making the buy, the "helpers" who had been standing in the background all turned around to show the big yellow "FBI" letters on the backs of their jackets, and the guy was busted. We took photos, tagged it, did a piece count, and loaded the clothes into the truck and into storage for the next seven months while the case wound its way through the courts.

REPORTING

Reports for intellectual property investigations are narrative in form, outlining how the merchandise was discovered, how it was verified as counterfeit, and so on. It's always a good idea to take as many photos of the merchandise as possible to augment the written report. Each photo has to be identified and described in the report, as they may be included as exhibits in a court case down the road.

PRICING AND PROFITABILITY

Intellectual property investigations pay well, and a couple of agencies have become very successful specializing in the field almost exclusively. Of course, much depends on the market; there is a lot of counterfeit merchandise floating around New York and LA, much less in Fargo and Dayton. The lead investigator can get fees of $85 to $95 per hour, depending on the market, for field investigative services, and up to $2,000 per week for undercover work. Taggers and counters (often secretaries or other clerical workers on the PI's staff) can get $10 to $12 per hour. Then there can be auxiliary billing for such tasks as title searches and background checks.

The larger the bust, the bigger the fee. While a simple serving of a cease and desist notice can generate about $250 in billing, a large case involving significant quantities of imported or domestically manufactured merchandise can bring in tens of thousands of dollars. The investigator can bill for serving as a liaison with law enforcement, conducting controlled buys, monitoring seizures, and even counting and tagging. If the case ends up in court, witness testimony can also be billable. In large cases, the hours can add up rapidly. Again, because raids and seizures frequently involve two or more trademark holders, billing is divided proportionally according to piece counts recovered or destroyed.

65

When law enforcement agencies get involved in these cases, the client knows that they do not send bills. You do, so make sure the client expects a timely invoice for the work you do in support of and cooperation with law enforcement. Again, counting and tagging does not require investigative expertise and therefore should be billed at a lesser (high-level clerical) rate. On the other hand, your time as an investigator, even if you were just drinking coffee with FBI Special Agents before the raid, should be billed at your rate.

Your client should be informed that your bill will be coming and when it does, it should detail exactly what it is for. Ask for payment upon receipt, and make sure it doesn't get stale. When the case is hot, you are valuable. Three months down the road, they will have trouble remembering what you did. More on this in Chapter 10.

With the right contacts, a professional approach, and good common sense, it's possible to make a lucrative career from IP investigations alone. Don't neglect this often overlooked field of private investigation.

Ch apter 8
Corporate Investigations

Corporate investigations can be hard to define, as it is an extremely broad category of PI work. Private companies have a significant and growing need for private investigators. In reality, the different services that can be provided to companies by PIs are limited only by one's imagination. We'll review just some of them here.

EMPLOYEE DISHONESTY

This is an enormous category. Law enforcement is completely overtaxed to provide much in the way of police work for cases of embezzlement and employee theft. And, with all due respect, many police departments have little or no experience dealing with white-collar crime. Indeed, many PDs may not consider white-collar crime to be all that serious. Possibly not when compared to murders and rapes, but white-collar crime can undercut the economy, cause businesses to go under, put innocent people out of work, and destroy futures and families.

This type of investigative work falls into two broad categories: detection and prevention. We'll look at each separately.

Detection Services

Companies are constantly plagued by dishonest and/or disruptive employees who steal product, money, or time. When a problem is suspected, either through employee tips, internal audit information showing unusual shortages, or simply realizing that product is missing or work isn't getting done, corporate executives will quickly learn that they will receive little or no assistance from law enforcement. Without the services of an internal security or loss-prevention department, there is nowhere else to turn for help except to private eyes. The expertise and capability of the PI determines how to approach the issue, whether through surveillance, undercover work, shopping services, interviews/interrogations, hidden cameras, or other investigative means.

For example, let's say a retail store suffers the disappearance of a cash deposit. The straightforward approach is for the investigator to determine who may have had access to the money, search for motive (financially burdened employees, grudges, etc.), then conduct interviews to obtain the facts of the case, read body language, look for inconsistencies and lies, and establish clear suspects. We often get admissions with this approach, but it takes real expertise in the art and science of interrogation and interview. Along the way, the PI must also recognize and highlight policy and procedure violations or other problems, which makes the investigation valuable for the client on still another level.

Another approach is through standard surveillance methods. A difficult and learned science, surveillance is a necessary arrow in the PI's investigative quiver. It can reveal all kinds of issues: romantic liaisons on company time, reckless driving, theft off loading and shipping docks, executive espionage of proprietary information, drinking and substance abuse during lunches and breaks, and on and on. Photos and video, of course, are mandatory.

We did a case once where the company—a manufacturer of windows and casements—was afraid there was some theft involving its delivery people. We set up a mobile surveillance team and followed the lead driver. Instead of going to his first stop, he went to a diner, where two other drivers (off route) met up with him and had breakfast for 45 minutes. Then the subject of the surveillance made a couple of legitimate deliveries, then stopped and had a 45 minute lunch, after which he pulled the truck behind the restaurant and promptly took a nap. (We took pictures through the windshield from the front bumper.) After his hour-long slumber, he made a couple more deliveries and then went car shopping, parking the delivery truck in front of a couple of dealers.

It turned out that the three drivers had conspired to generate overtime pay by deliberate slowdowns and wasting time. They all had been doing this for so long that the length of the trips appeared to be normal. The bogus overtime was costing the company hundreds of thousands of dollars a year, far more than any theft that was occurring. When confronted, one of the newer drivers told of being physically threatened if he did not go along with the scheme. GPS tracking is now a good way of stopping this kind of theft, but we cracked the case the old-fashioned way—with mobile surveillance, photographic evidence, and detailed reporting.

Prevention Services

Many, many companies have a steady and real need for a resourceful, responsive PI who can augment or actually replace the in-house loss-prevention director if the services provided not only detect and eliminate problems but also proscribe prevention actions that can eliminate issues before they arise. These can include such services as pre-employment background checks, loss-prevention surveys of equipment or information, recommendations to improve internal policies and procedures, and physical security. Also, seminars and meetings can increase employee awareness of the issue, making honest employees more proactive in the loss-prevention function. Making recommendations for better computer security, educating supervisors on what clues to watch for, and conducting exit interviews of departing employees are all preventive services the investigator can provide that are not only helpful to the client but also to the success of the investigator. Tying up a case of a dishonest employee, with specific recommendations to prevent it from happening in the future, can solidify that PI's position with the client company and provide work for years to come.

SEXUAL HARASSMENT

Sexual harassment investigations are always sensitive, and because most incidents of a sexual nature are fairly private, they frequently come down to a case of "he said, she said." Further, most claims of sexual harassment point upward—that is, a subordinate is having problems with a supervisor or member of management. It is, therefore, very smart on the part of corporate executives to hire out independent, unbiased investigative support to determine the facts behind a sexual harassment complaint.

One of the silliest actions I've seen time and time again is a reluctance of the investigator to be blunt and forthright in questioning and reporting. Because many sexual incidents fall into gray areas, the investigator cannot be embarrassed to ask very direct questions if he or she is going to get to the truth of the matter. Touching, for example, is very different if done on the arm than on the breast. The specifics must be clear. If an accuser won't give specifics, perhaps there are none.

I've investigated dozens of complaints over the years, and I've seen a myriad of motives for sexual harassment charges. Many had little or nothing to do with sex. In any event, investigating charges of sexual harassment in the workplace is a good niche business.

EMPLOYEE PERFORMANCE

Employees who do some or all of their work off premises, such as salesmen, repairmen, and deliverymen, sometimes do things they are not supposed to do. This can range from simply not working when they are supposed to be, to working improperly, to doing things that endanger the reputation or liability of the company. Therefore, it is a common practice for companies to use PIs to tail their employees for legitimate purpose. This can take the form of traditional surveillance or even via such high-tech methods as attaching a GPS tracking unit to a company vehicle.

INDUSTRIAL ESPIONAGE

The theft of sensitive and proprietary information continues to grow at an alarming rate, especially in high-tech industries. Investigations to uncover industrial espionage can involve researching the suspect's financial records to reveal assets in excess of income. Surveillance to identify his or her contacts and actions might be called for, but because the espionage takes place intermittently, usually over a long period of time, surveillance can go on for weeks, and the investigator must be prepared to have the resources to conduct it. Undercover investigators might be used to ingratiate themselves with the suspect. Sometimes using an attractive female or male agent in the classic "honey trap" works well, as people who perpetrate these kinds of actions have a tendency to brag about it.

Very few PIs specialize in this kind of investigation, and it's usually authorized at the highest level—and brings in the highest fees.

BUSINESS INTELLIGENCE

Another specialized skill, and one that can be extremely lucrative, is gathering business intelligence. This is a learned field, requiring more than instincts alone. You must be able to analyze the target company's marketing strategies, determine sales by distribution networks and activity, profile the principals of the company, and monitor a whole laundry list of business areas that can be useful to your client. With the right kind of information gathering and analysis, one can determine the trends and culture of a company, estimate its financial strength, and even forecast research and development of new products. Much of this can be done on the Internet—a gold mine of information if you know where to look beyond the company's Web site—but traditional methods of information gathering, such as old-fashioned surveillance or pretext interviews, are often needed to get the inside stuff.

REPORTING

As always, constant and timely dissemination of information is crucial. Corporate executives, even those who live vicariously through the private eye, have little time to wade through meaningless reports. On the other hand, reports must provide all details, be vivid in their conclusions, and usually provide recommendations for prevention of problems in the future.

Narrative reports for corporate investigations are mandatory. Let's break down the components of a typical corporate report.

Case Summary

This paragraph is a brief description of how the case was started and a general outline of the plan of attack. It tells the client what you are investigating and what actions are anticipated. For example:

"Client's internal audit determined an apparent variance in cash deposits made on consecutive dates during the previous month. In response to these variances, it was decided to initiate an investigation to determine the circumstances surrounding the apparent cash shortages. Anticipated measures to be included in this investigation are background investigations of all persons deemed to have access to the cash deposits, a review of the procedures and physical security of the cash deposit systems, and interviews with all persons with possible knowledge of or involvement in the apparent cash shortages."

Case Facts

This section details the specifics of the case. Following the above example, you would list the dates of the cash shortages and the names of persons on duty and/or with access to the cash on those dates. List any historical information, such as previous similar situations, and the chain of custody of the deposits (such as from the store to the courier to the bank).

Case Investigation

This section details the meat of the investigation. It outlines the facts found during the background investigations, provides details about any interviews conducted, and reviews physical security and/or cash-handling procedures. Subtopics under this heading would include the individual interviews of persons identified to have had access to the missing money, identified by each person's name and job title. Either entire transcripts or pertinent details from the interviews are given, with emphasis on any admissions or incriminations. In a separate summation of each interview, the investigator would give his opinion as to the veracity of the responses, indications of attempts at deception, and any other opinions and/or subjective comments.

Case Conclusion

This section details your findings and conclusions. If you solve the case, especially if you are able to obtain admissions, either verbal or in writing, don't hesitate to give yourself enough credit. Often, clients will not understand how difficult it is to actually solve a crime. Having been weaned on movies and television, they expect cases to be solved in an hour or two, neatly wrapped up before the commercials. So make sure the client understands the amount of work, insight, and expertise you put into the investigation.

If the case is not solved, list opinions and conclusions along with any and all supporting evidence. Do not accuse without reasonable grounds. The phrase "probable cause" is a good one to remember when presenting your conclusions, because it does not mean guilt but just the possibility that guilt exists. (In other words, it is a good way to express your opinion that the guy is guilty without saying he is.) Any unproven suspicions must be identified as such, with verbiage such as, "It is the opinion of this investigator, given the information available at this time, that 'Subject X' may have direct responsibility for (or 'knowledge of') the missing $2,000."

Recommendations

This section of a report can rescue a go-nowhere investigation. Even if you don't solve the crime, almost every investigation will turn up deficiencies and problems with internal policies and procedures. Specific recommendations to identify and fix problems can make your report to management invaluable, even if you haven't solved the original case. Therefore, always ask interviewees how they feel about the company, if they are aware of any problems, who they think is a poor employee, and so on. Loss of cash or merchandise often results from a breakdown in procedures or a lack of procedures. Stepping a little into the consultant's role can make an investigative report extremely valuable and ensure repeat business.

PRICING AND PROFITABILITY

Corporate work is growing tremendously throughout the private sector and should be strongly considered as an avenue to success for the investigator. A polished, professional image is, of course, necessary, as companies have learned to shy away from the thug-like investigator with the bulge under his jacket and the sap in his back pocket. A suit and tie and briefcase are now the standard image, and the investigator needs to be able to interact with executives at the highest level and address their needs with an eye to improving their (and your) bottom line.

Your hourly rate will depend on the type and difficultly of the case and the depth of the pockets of the company you are working for. Retailers, for example, will expect fees just a little north of $60 per hour, while you can usually bill manufacturers at a rate of $95 to $125 per hour. Financial service companies will expect that and more—don't be afraid to ask for $125 to $150 an hour if you get complicated cases in that sector.

Surveillance rates can also vary. If the surveillance is long—say a week or more—you will bill at a volume rate of around $50 to $60 per hour. If it's a day or so, ask for $85 to $95 an hour.

If you are good at interrogations and frequently get admissions, your rate should be $110 to $125 an hour. If it's a routine interview as part of an investigation, you'll have to bill less; $65 per hour is normal, especially if there are several interviews to do.

Some PIs, after establishing a strong rapport with a company and being considered the "company guy," will send invoices for flat amounts for "services rendered." Obviously, this will give you some space for upper-level billing.

Don't forget small add-ons that can help your bottom line immensely. Set-up and administration fees of $20 to $50 are common and not usually questioned by corporate accounts-payable people.

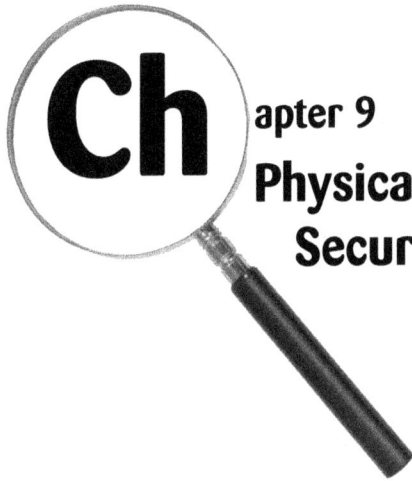

Ch apter 9
Physical and Personal Security Work

There is a clear distinction between performing investigations and providing on-site or personal security, but I will discuss security work here because many investigators get into it, and many security professionals get into investigations.

In general, successful investigations depend on how many things you do right; successful security—whether it's physical security of a location, or personal security for individuals—depends on how few things you do wrong. In other words, good security hinges on anticipating what could go wrong, then taking steps to prevent it.

ON-SITE SECURITY

Security is linked with investigations in the public's mind, so when an investigator does a good job for a company, the client will sometimes look to him or her for physical security as well. We're talking about the uniformed security force that controls access to the building, patrols the premises, monitors security cameras, and so forth.

A good investigator can usually run a good security shop; a good security officer can rarely be a good investigator. This is because the thought processes, creativity, and old-fashioned savvy required for private investigation generally are not prerequisites for manning a security post or making nightly rounds. However, sometimes a diamond can be found in the rough. We've found excellent undercover investigators in security officer uniforms.

That said, all the characteristics of a good soldier apply to a good security officer, including:

- Sharp appearance and demeanor
- Pride in oneself and the job
- Strong discipline and dedication to duty
- Attention to detail
- Alert and competent

Because of this, military training can make for excellent background in security work.

The keys to good security are establishing good procedures and following them repeatedly. This is accomplished through training and communication and more training and communication. Each site should have written "post orders," or a description of all the duties and responses to emergencies the security officers must do. These written orders should be discussed in detail with the officers so there are no questions. Then, continuous and random spot checks must be done to the site.

One of the most important functions of a security officer is to keep good records in the form of a log and incident reports. If anything happens, the first thing any attorney will ask for is the records. If thorough, current records are not kept, it may be impossible to show you are not negligent. The officer must keep daily logs of all activities, including roving patrols, receipt of visitors, and so forth. Whenever a security supervisor visits the site, separate entries (usually in red) must be made to the log. In addition, the officer must make out separate incident reports of any occurrence that may be out of the ordinary. These can cover everything from discovered safety and security hazards to unexplained packages, suspicious strangers, and so on. Both logs and incidents reports must be stored and available for at least five years.

Anyone going into the security business must be aware of the direction of the industry. There is a huge consolidation drive by the large security companies, which is putting a real squeeze on the small guys. Big companies can offer things the little guy can't, like extensive fringe benefits, better training programs, and opportunities for growth. However, a local PI branching off into the security business can make up ground with a level of personalized service the big firms can't match. All and all, however, going into the security business these days is a fairly tough road. But if a niche is established, a decent living can be made—and, of course, there is always the possibility that a big outfit will come along and absorb your niche business, with a tidy little buyout price for you.

EXECUTIVE PROTECTION
AND EXECUTIVE ASSISTANCE

In the horse and buggy days, this used to be called bodyguarding. This service has matured away from the stereotypical goon who offers protection by cracking the head of anyone coming close to his "package." Some celebrities still like having the monster wrestler to clear away crowds and provide protection, but I suspect that this has as much to do with ego and image than actual direct protection.

Today's protection specialist is a true professional who approaches the job with extreme preparation, planning, research, and common sense. Further, he (and, in many cases, she) is highly trained. In fact, do not even attempt to enter the field without good previous training—military, law enforcement, or otherwise. Former Secret Service agents and Special Ops military personnel such as SEALs and Green Berets often make excellent protection/assistance people; weightlifters, pro wrestlers, and bouncers do not.

Real protection these days is accomplished through brains, not brawn. While basic hand-to-hand combat, firearm use, and other defensive measures are important, there is much more to the profession than that. One also needs to be skilled in such areas as surveillance and countersurveillance, evasive driving techniques, land navigation, languages, emergency medical procedures, and even social etiquette. A pleasing personality is necessary, as is a command presence and a professional demeanor. Muscle shirts are a no-no; suits and ties are the uniform. Shoes must be businesslike, yet supple enough for quick movements and stability. Weapons are never seen. The last thing a protection specialist wants to do is draw attention to himself and the client. The specialist knows that if he or she has to brandish or use a weapon, they've failed in the mission.

One thing that is certain about every client is that they will always do what they wish, so the protection specialist must be flexible yet work within the needed security parameters. These parameters require specialized and intimate knowledge of such things as:

- The needs, traits, and quirks of the client.
- The geography, access and egress routes, landmarks, and even the culture of the area of operation.
- Local law enforcement, to include standard laws, key personnel, and liaison officers.
- Availability of supplies and equipment, such as vehicles and other means of transportation, medical equipment, communication gear, etc.

Any protection assignment requires meticulous prior planning to learn all the above and to try to anticipate the unexpected. A detailed plan must be developed, then presented and discussed with the client to establish good communication and a sense of confidence. A genuine rapport must be developed so that constant cooperation exists. In fact, the profession has evolved to such a degree that most assignments are now called "executive assistance," as the protection specialist may be required to provide all kinds of support, from finding today's copy of the *Wall Street Journal* to theater tickets to good tables in the best restaurants. The protection part is woven into the assisting part, with the assistance often being first and most important.

There are packs of people chasing this business, and assignments are sporadic at best. But if a client or two is scored, it can be quite lucrative. Whereas a security officer may be billed out at around $15 to $17 an hour, a protection specialist will charge $95 to $125 an hour. For extended assignments (which may last up to a year or more), a flat rate is negotiated. Numbers well into six figures per year, plus expenses, are not uncommon.

While the work often has dry spells, some details can be around the clock for several days, and the hours will add up. Then there is the prospect of international work, which can have an entirely different and higher compensation rate. International protection gets a higher rate because it is usually more dangerous (think kidnappings, roadside bombings, etc.); entails specialized knowledge of the culture, terrain, and language; and often requires a local contact.

In my opinion, the best clients are top executives; minor celebrities are the worst. We did some protection for actor Matt Damon, and he couldn't have been better. Others haven't been so good, particularly egocentric, finicky, and self-impressed B-level celebs. Businesspeople will listen to common sense and be cooperative because they understand the mission. Some media types never get it, and the specialist ends up being an expensive babysitter, sometimes protecting other people from the client.

Protection service has extended into ordinary businesses, where the possibility of workplace violence is present. These days, when a belligerent or dangerous employee is being terminated, protection people are sometimes brought in to maintain order. Usually, their presence is enough of a deterrent, so no problems arise. Security professionals have also been called on for things like legal proceedings, stockholder's meetings when things are not going so well, and other instances where the potential for conflict exists. Generally, the most important part of this service is the peace of mind the protection specialist brings to the floor.

As with most investigative and security services, common sense, awareness, and quick thinking are essential traits when it comes to working as a protection specialist. But that is not enough; proper, formal training in personal security is required by the client more often than not. You can protect some people with the basic traits of an investigator, but if you think you want to be a true professional, seek qualified training. There are two or three excellent schools in the country, well worth the money if you are going to be serious. Some schools offer two-day courses for under $500, plus travel expenses, which provide a solid first step for the aspiring protection specialist. Such courses won't make you an expert, but they might help you make contacts in the industry and get your foot in the door.

Chapter 10
Running Your Business

In some ways, private investigators are similar to computer programmers—they are excellent with the process but horrible businesspeople. Over the years, I've seen every example of business incompetence imaginable and the demise of a large number of agencies. I've seen investigators who shot themselves in the foot (literally, playing with a weapon in the office); ran their business from the trunk of their car, with tennis racquets, sleeping bags, and trash mixed in with cash and company files; and accidentally fed checks for services through a shredder.

There are reasons for this. A lot has to do with the nature of the people who enter this line of work, in that most private eyes would rather be sleuthing than sitting behind a desk pushing papers. Also, it happens to be a difficult business. You are not inventorying widgets on a shelf and selling them retail. Much of the business is non-repetitive—that is, it's one case at a time, which you work to its conclusion before moving on to the next one. It is difficult to market and sell yourself, and there is much competition.

PROFESSIONAL PITFALLS

Yet given all of the natural enemies to a successful business, private detectives still fall prey to self-inflicted wounds. One of the most common is what I call the "war story syndrome." Investigative work uncovers the best and worst in human behavior, and the private eye will work on cases that make for great cocktail party patter. Rather than taking care of business, however, PIs will spend excessive time sitting around and telling stories of previous cases and triumphs. They need to get over it and get to business.

Another big one is having too many people on staff. Without question, to do the business you need good people. And it takes some doing to find, hire, and train those good people. But if you don't have the business, you can't afford the people. The trap is that you bring on good people to handle cases and earn money. If and when the caseload drops, you still are paying those people but they are earning little or no money.

This can be hard to discern. There is an old adage that says, "People will use the amount of work they have to fit the amount of time they have." What this means is that an investigator may be working on 10 cases or two, but he will seem just as busy in either case, and it will take just as long to do the two cases as the 10. Often the investigator himself doesn't realize the drop in productivity. So stay lean at the top. Payroll will kill you.

Another major pitfall? The paperwork gets the lowest priority. A successful agency makes the paperwork the most important aspect of the business. After all, what is the investigator's product? It's information. And how does that product get sold? By disseminating that information to clients in the form of reports. How do you get paid for your product? By giving your client a bill (and collecting that bill) for services rendered. All of this requires paperwork. Movie and TV detectives always seem to work for free. They certainly never do paperwork. That may be great to keep the plot moving along, but it stinks for staying in business and paying the rent.

When I first started out, I worked for a PI in New York named Erwin who amazed me daily. He would see things that I missed entirely. I often didn't believe him, but he was never wrong. And he was one of the best natural interrogators I ever met. He learned the trade from his father, who had a New York agency for some 40 years.

The son (my boss) was at the time the youngest licensed PI in the state of New York. He had some of the most prestigious clients in the city. He had a great reputation for detecting and dealing with employee theft. The problem was that, although he always had good office space, he usually worked out of the trunk of his car. In fact, when you opened the truck, it was filled to the brim with notes, reports, recording and viewing gear, changes of clothes, sporting equipment, and, buried at the bottom, even large amount of loose cash.

The result? Reports to clients were always late. Invoices to clients were always late. In fact, he would often forget to send *any* bill for much of his work. He was always on the verge of success but never got there because, as mentioned, he was the stereotypical private eye—always in the field, always into the cases, and always bouncing from one to another. In the end, he was totally incapable of working for anyone and lived like a hired gun from the Old West—going in, getting the job done, and riding off into the sunset. How many times have you seen cowboys write reports and send bills? How many rich cowboys have you seen?

Suffice to say, Erwin's success was limited. I must say, he had a great time and every day was an adventure, but he never rose above just making a living. Of course, if you look around and throw out Julius Kroll and a few others, the PIs who have *really* made it are few. But taking care of business is the foundation of success at any level, and the foundation of taking care of business is good paperwork.

LICENSING AND INSURANCE

To be a real private eye, you have to be licensed as such. Occasionally I run into guys who just start doing the work, without bothering to get legal. They are always yahoos who invariably get into trouble fast.

Every state requires a degree of experience to become a licensed PI, and some require passing a written exam. The experience can come from work as a law-enforcement officer or with an established agency. States are usually pretty liberal about the experience issue— if it seems legit, it will usually pass through unquestioned.

The tests are another matter. Don't pass, no license, no kidding. The questions are mostly on laws pertaining to the conduct of PIs, but don't think you can walk though the test without being prepared. Study for them, and use the manuals the state will provide.

Fees to stay licensed vary from state to state. Expect to pay a sizable first-year fee, followed by annual renewal fees.

Insurance is crucial, as we live in an intensely litigious culture, and you will invariably annoy the person you are investigating. The annoyed person will often contact an attorney who will work on anything that has a contingency fee attached. Protect yourself with insurance. I recommend a minimum coverage of $1 million per incident, $3 million aggregate. Three to five million in coverage is not excessive these days.

Insurance is expensive, so shop around. Brownyard Group specializes in investigator and security liability insurance and is a good place to start. You can find them on the Web.

REPORTS

Your product is information. Intelligence. The packaging is reports. Getting the information is usually hard, and it is never enough. When you do get information, whether it is a dishonest employee detected, assets found, a missing person located, or a background profiled, you must provide it in a clear, intelligent, and professional written report. PIs usually puff up with success when they get the information, forgetting that information in a vacuum is worth very little. It has to be processed, verified, and disseminated. *Then* it has value. Then you can send a bill and (hopefully) get paid.

PIs often crank out reports that look like they've been in a dry cleaning bag for two weeks. I've learned that it is well worth the relatively minimal added cost to produce a report on solid paper stock (rather than ordinary copy paper) and have it professionally bound in a sleek cover. To obtain the best price, the report has to look attractive, be timely (being late can completely devalue the information), and, above all, contain accurate and complete information. I've seen too many reports that ask more questions than they answer. The gospel rule of answering who, what, when, where, why, and how must be factored into each and every report. And it has to be literate (with spell and grammar checks available on most computers, there is no excuse for misspelled words or fractured language), direct, and concise.

You can be creative with format, as long as it's concise and professional. We've found that, except for mystery shopping reports, check-off forms are no replacement for the narrative report. You have a story to tell, so tell it well and accurately. After a lot of different tries, we ended up using the following format for most of our investigative reports.

We start with the heading, which identifies the client and the location of the investigation. It also includes the date, case number, and identity of the investigator. The narrative begins with a "Case Initiation" paragraph. This lists the reasons for the investigation, includes any lead-in information, and reviews what the investigation is targeted to do. Then, to have the biggest impact, we follow with a "Summary" paragraph outlining the information found and results of the investigation. This section would give your conclusions and what you believe are the results of your efforts. Following this will be the meat of your report, titled according to what you did (for example, "Interview: Joe Doe," or simply "Investigation" or "Surveillance").

Once again, there must be scrupulous attention to accuracy. The defense against libel is the truth, so the truth is what should be reported. Speculation and opinion should be identified as such. Rather than calling a person guilty if it is not or cannot be proved, it's best to say something like, "It is recommended that Subject X not be eliminated from suspicion for involvement in or knowledge of the [investigated incident(s)] with information available at this time."

BILLING, CASH FLOW, AND COLLECTIONS

Getting paid is one of the most difficult, if not the most difficult part of the business. There are a lot of reasons for this. On the most fundamental level, it comes down to a short memory on the part of the client. When you are desperately needed by the client, you are the savior. When you are done saving their profits or even their business itself and they don't need you anymore, paying you is the last thing they have on their mind. (Saying that, there are a lot of honorable companies and people out there who will pay, and pay in a timely manner.)

Amongst this minefield are some special areas of concern. The first is domestic cases. People who hire you for primarily emotional reasons cannot always be trusted to do the right thing. They will call and badger you daily while you are helping their agenda, then disappear when it's over. Always, always work against a fat retainer when taking on a domestic. Make sure the upfront money exceeds what you have to put into the case, if possible. If they have the money, they'll give it to you up front. If they don't have the money up front, chances are they won't have it after you finish the job. You can always take a credit card; it's the easiest way to proceed, and you get your money right away.

Then there's lawyers. The worst. They expect timely payment from their clients but find no moral compulsion to pay you for legitimate services rendered. Be wary when working for attorneys, and make it a point to ask early and often for your money. It doesn't matter if you are dealing with a large and prestigious firm or a single personal injury ambulance chaser—it's usually tough to get paid.

Oddly, PIs will often do a fabulous job, sometimes even a miraculous job, then not bother to send a bill for a long time (sometimes never). If the written report is the PI's product, the invoice is his or her lifeblood. Put together a professional format for your invoice and send it out with the report. Some tips:

▶ Make your bill "payable upon receipt." If you do not get paid within 15 days, start calling. If there's no check within 30 days, call with urgency, and follow up a couple days later with a letter detailing your concern. No check within 45 days, call the client and tell him you'll be by to pick it up.

▶ Charge interest on overdue bills. Any simple accounting software, such as QuickBooks, will automatically add interest to outstanding receivables. Set up an automatic system and follow it.

▶ Be prepared for bad debts. People hate to pay lawyers, dentists, and . . . private eyes. Whenever possible, get your money up front as a retainer and, whenever possible, get cash. Find a good collections attorney in case you have to turn the bill over for collection.

▶ Have two kinds of invoices—the real one and a washed, "virgin" bill that does not list the specific services rendered. Why? Oftentimes the client needs complete discretion and does not want accounts payable to know what they are paying for. For example, the real bill may say, "Surveillance: Mortimer Snerd—10 hours at $85 per hour: $850." Mortimer may be an executive of the company, and the president may not want anyone else to know he is being followed. So you have to cleanse the information off the bill. The washed bill may read, "Consulting Services Rendered—$850." We've even set up a fictitious company simply to bill covertly. A generic name such as "Andrews Sales Company" can send bills for a variety of innocuous reasons. Of course, you will have to set up multiple checking accounts, with common signatories, to deposit and cash the checks.

▶ Make sure your invoice is simple, well organized, and professional in appearance. Above all, make sure it is accurate. Clients often have a built-in prejudice that the PI will pad the bill. Don't make them right. Cheating, even a little, can kill you down the road.

YOUR OFFICE

Private investigators work out of their office, home, car, or back pocket. From where you launch your investigations will depend on where you are in your career, how much money you wish to spend, and what return you are looking for. Certainly a posh office is nice, but the cost comes off the bottom line and therefore out of your pocket. On the other hand, you can set up your car with almost everything you need and save a lot of money, but you'll fall into that category of detective who's never really made it and is viewed with a touch of sleaze. Therefore, make careful decisions on where you want to set up shop and what good it will do for you.

Equipment

Regardless where you work, there are certain pieces of equipment that you must have. This starts (and ends) with a high-end laptop computer. With this one piece of equipment, you can find information, keep track of your cases, do your billing and bookkeeping, and write your reports. You cannot exist as a working PI without one, so spend the money on a good one and keep up to date with the technology. Mate it with a high-quality laser printer. Color is nice to have but not essential. Make sure your printer can also function as a fax machine. Getting one that serves as a photocopier and scanner is handy as well.

The computer gives you access to the Internet, which in turn gives you access to an astounding amount of information. Appendix D contains a listing of good online sources of information, but beware: these can change overnight. Build a binder of information sources, and update it weekly. It will serve as your foundation for online information gathering.

You will need an excellent, long-play tape recorder. Make sure it has a jack for an external microphone, is voice activated, and has good sensitivity.

You will need cameras, of course, and they'll need to be digital. Learn to transmit photos via e-mail; it has a tremendous impact on the appearance of your reports. Learn to use a telephoto lens. Make sure your cell phone can also take and send photos. This can be very important for cases such as intellectual property investigations, where you might have to take pictures surreptitiously. Taking some quick cell-phone snapshots of counterfeit clothing to send to your "wife" for her opinion is a more convincing pretext than whipping out a digital camera in the middle of a store and photographing racks of illegal merchandise. The latter will almost certainly make the storeowner nervous; the former, coupled with convincing acting, will seem like routine stuff.

Binoculars. Have a couple of pairs; one pocket sized and one for the car or static surveillances. Night-vision gear used to be outrageously expensive, but not anymore. It is a good investment if surveillances are your thing.

A camcorder. Make sure it has a stabilization feature and the telephoto lens is at least 10 power. Forget digital zoom—optical zoom is what you want. Also, it's important to be able to cut off the audio. I can't tell you the level of embarrassment you'll experience when you show a client a videotape and there is surveillance chatter on top of it. There is no shortage of four-letter words in the world of private investigations, and the camcorder will capture every one of them for your client's enjoyment later. I once had an investigator on surveillance who did not know that his camcorder automatically embedded cute little icons on the tape to coincide with holidays. When the tape of the bad guy filling up the trunk of his car was shown to the client, there was a dopey little pumpkin saying "Happy Halloween" in the corner of the images. Not professional.

Get a pocket day timer with room for quick notes. With that, you can't have enough pens in handy places. It's very embarrassing to whip out your day timer in front of a new client to take down the details about a potential case, only to have to borrow his pen.

Personal digital assistants, universally known as PDAs, can make your life much easier. It won't take long to accumulate an extended list of important phone numbers that you have to carry with you. If you are successful, you'll have to keep track of many appointments. Notes, tasks, and memos accumulate fast. Access to the Internet while in the field can provide crucial information right when you need it. All of this can be available to you with a good PDA such as a BlackBerry.

If you're doing surveillances, especially long ones such as investigating workman's comp fraud, put together a kit for the car. Included should be a change of clothes, different jackets and hats, nonprescription glasses—anything to alter your appearance. The kit should also include a small cooler for food and drinks, a container to pee in, as well as your basic surveillance gear.

Also consider fake business cards that provide you with a bit of innocuous cover should your presence in an area ever be challenged. Have it read something like "Water Table Research" or "Public Property Inspector" that will give you a plausible reason to be hanging around. Use a gender-neutral name such as "Lee Edwards" or "Robin Cutler" so the cards can be used by male or female investigators. You can subscribe to a cover phone line for the number listed on the card that will not come up on caller ID and will let you set your own voice mail.

Don't be afraid of high-tech tools that can make your job easier. GPS tracking devices, for example, have come down drastically in price and will pay for themselves in no time. Surf the Net and you'll find more than a couple of sources for these products. Some units are attached to a vehicle, then removed and plugged into your computer for the report. Others allow you to track live from your computer. The latter is better because the risk of detection comes with placing and removing the equipment. You also run the risk of violating trespass laws if you attach these things to a subject's car on someone else's property. Tracking the spouse of the owner of the car gives you free latitude to place the device, as you have permission to do so. If you don't have permission, you can be arrested for trespassing, so don't do it. But if you can do it legally, go with GPS tracking technology. It saves you and your client money, eliminates getting blown on surveillance, and provides excellent information.

Firearms

This is an interesting area. Most TV and movie PIs carry guns around, not to mention use them to shoot a lot of bad guys. Needless to say, TV and movies are not real life. Packing a pistol may seem glamorous, and usually the first question you get from the blank-eyed blonde at a cocktail party is, "Do you have a gun?" But remember, while there is a certain cachet in carrying a piece, there is also a large portion of danger and stupidity.

Discharging a weapon anywhere, anytime, carries an enormous liability. Even simply displaying one can have serious legal ramifications. I've known PIs (more than one) who have literally shot themselves in the foot while fooling around with their guns. And you really have to ask yourself, "Would I ever shoot someone?" If the answer is (hopefully) "no," you'll find that there are few times, if ever, when you will really need a firearm. Personal weapons should be for personal protection only—never to impress someone, never to intimidate someone, and certainly never to harm someone other than in justifiable self-defense. Remember:

> ▶ If you fire a weapon, you will have to provide very good reason why you did so. Most of the time it will be judged to be irresponsible and will put your license and career in jeopardy.

▸ If you wound someone, you'll undoubtedly be sued and possibly be criminally charged as well. (That's right, killing someone is usually cheaper than wounding them.)

▸ If you are not an expert in handling a firearm, and I mean truly an expert, you always run the risk of it being taken away and used on you. This happens even to experienced police officers.

▸ If you forget you are carrying it around and wind up in a place where you are not authorized to carry, you may be criminally charged. Courthouses, police departments, some public places like malls, even certain communities take a dim view of people carrying guns into their areas.

If you feel you have good reason to carry a firearm, don't do so until after you've undergone realistic training with a qualified instructor. Then apply for a concealed carry permit in your state. Only carry a gun when there is a clear and present danger to yourself, such as when you have to operate in dangerous neighborhoods or stake out someone with documented violent tendencies. Never flash it around or use it as an intimidation device. Show a weapon while you are doing an interrogation and it is a sure way to have any statement you get from the subject disqualified as "obtained under duress."

Guns are not toys. They are used to kill people. That is not good for business. Best advice is stay away from them as much as possible.

STAFF

Employees are by far the most expensive pieces of equipment. The temptation is to bring people on board to help with investigations. This is natural because, after all, the only way you earn money is if a human being does something. So, the logic is that if I can earn $800 a day, and my assistant, to whom I pay $300 a day, earns the same, I can get an extra $500 for myself.

The theory looks perfect; the reality is something else again. What new PIs don't often take into consideration are the hidden costs of these extra investigators, such as taxes, insurance, and benefits. And, except for ongoing services such as employee screenings and mystery shopping surveys, all cases eventually end, and you have to get new cases to generate new revenue.

If you have investigators on staff, you must make marketing your highest priority so you can keep them productive. Marketing is not investigating, and it certainly does not earn money in of itself. So sometimes when you think you will be earning more money by having more investigators, you will in fact be earning less.

The rule of thumb is that you should be billing three times what you are paying out in payroll. And your employees should have an 80 percent productivity rate. That is to say, they should be earning rather than costing you money. I've seen too many good agencies go under because of the payroll burden. An occupational hazard is to tell war stories in the office while drinking coffee and waiting for the phone to ring. It won't take long for any profits to be eaten up by payroll costs.

And consider your support staff. Every PI loves the thought of having a luscious receptionist answering calls and taking care of all needs. But that person doesn't earn any revenue, and the salary you actually pay costs you about 25 to 30 percent more when you factor in the hidden costs. Same goes for typists and gofers.

On the other hand, one person can only do so much. So if you are interested in making more than just a living, you will have to have some employees, and you will have to learn to organize, delegate, market, and manage, just like any business.

Which leads to the issue of your identity. Are you a big-time, big-deal private eye or a struggling businessman? They are two distinctly different breeds, and it is difficult, if not impossible, for some people, to be both. A lot of the traits that make for a good investigator, such as aggression, a sense of adventure, and thinking outside the box, are exactly what can hurt the organizational businessman. Every successful PI eventually has to face this dilemma.

After a good reputation and track record are established, the time will come when expansion must be considered. It is best to anticipate these decisions and make sure they are carefully considered. Unfortunately, many PIs plunge ahead without deep thought as to where they are going and quickly get in over their heads. Remember, bigger is not necessarily better; better is better.

Chapter 11
Marketing
Your Business

I used to think marketing, in the classic sense, was close to impossible for a private investigation agency. You can't hang a sign out saying, "Get your detective, here!" with a giant arrow pointing at your office. But over the years I've learned that not only is marketing possible, it's mandatory.

Most investigative work is goal orientated; that is, you get a case, you solve a case. But where does the next case come from? Unless there is recurring work, such as ongoing shopping surveys or background investigations, there always needs to be something new coming your way. Even in the case of shopping services and background screenings, you are prey to the whims of the seasons, the economy, your client's budget, and the competition. Therefore, there is probably nothing more important to success (except, of course, for being a good investigator) than an ongoing marketing program. Here's how to do it.

PUBLIC RELATIONS

The best way to get business is to be famous. How do you get famous? By being out there, being visible, and using the media as much as possible. The public loves a good detective story, so if you have one, do your best to get it in the papers or, even better, on television. If you can afford it, hire a good public relations specialist to get stories planted in trade journals, magazines, and local papers. Contact local television and radio stations and let them know who you are and that you are available for talk shows. Offer to write articles, with real-life stories, for any paper or magazine you can find. Even letters to the editor under your name can help.

Join local professional organizations such as the chamber of commerce, Rotary Club, and Better Business Bureau. You may have to attend painfully boring breakfasts and lunches that seem to be a colossal waste of time, but every person you meet, every card you hand out, every hand you shake, is a potential client.

Polish up your public speaking skills and volunteer to give talks on anything you can think of: personal security, loss prevention, background investigations, locates, and so on. Spice it with good detective stories.

On top of that, get out on the town and meet people. Go to the hot bars, restaurants, and clubs. Get known in the best circles. When my agency was still young, I got more business from bars than the hundreds of direct mailings and phone calls I did. Think of such nationally famous PIs as Beau Deitl and Anthony Pelicano—they got to the top by being where the action was and being visible.

And never forget that there is a significant portion of showbiz to the image of the private eye. Cultivate an air of professionalism and success, but with a dash of mystery. Here are some do's and don'ts to achieving this:

Do:

▸ Dress business-like, with a touch (just a touch) of flamboyance. A navy pinstripe suit with a white shirt and a wild tie is an example. An expensive sport jacket with a black turtleneck is also a nice image. The trench coat is a must. Wear high-quality, thin-soled shoes.

▸ Have high-quality, professional business cards. My cards were gold on solid black, and they always made an impression.

▸ Join a country club or ritzy fitness club; it's a good way to network. A private eye can be low rent or on a par with attorneys, accountants, and other professionals. Obviously, the latter is better.

▶ Drive a car that fits the image. A 10-year-old Jaguar is much better than a brand new Buick station wagon.

▶ Carry yourself with pride. Stand straight, talk in a normal tone, and do not be either overly aggressive or passively quiet. Avoid at all costs the posture and body language of the sleazy gumshoe.

▶ Smile well and often.

▶ Be seen with attractive women; it adds to the mystique. If you can't get attractive, at least go for exotic.

▶ Have your phones answered by a female with a soft, sexy voice. It fits the image.

▶ Get the best address you can afford. Being convenient to the action and looking successful is important.

Don't:

▶ Be sloppy, unshaven, and rumpled. Colombo could get away with a wrinkled and battered raincoat, but that's television.

▶ Be loud and aggressive. You may think it scares the bad guys, but it only drives away clients and women.

▶ Wear tacky or excessive jewelry. It adds to the sleaze factor.

▶ Flaunt a weapon. It's stupid, bush league, and dangerous.

▶ Get arrested for anything. That includes motor vehicle violations. A PI without a car severely limits his surveillance ability.

▶ Eat and drink too much. A fat, drunk PI is the way it used to be, not now.

DIRECT MAIL

The traditional way to market yourself and your services is through direct mail. While it's frustratingly difficult to get a response, it still remains the best way to make potential clients aware of you and your agency. Don't forget, you are not selling a service but a name.

Painfully, you can only expect a response rate of 1 to 2 percent on your direct mail piece. Therefore, if you send out a hundred letters, you may generate one or two possibles. And even that thin success depends on the appearance and content of your letter and who receives it. Don't think you can send out 10 or 20 letters, then sit back and wait for the phone to ring.

To maximize your return rate, keep in mind the following tips:

▸ In the grand scheme of things, quality stationary is cheap. You can send a letter on inexpensive paper and save, what, perhaps $100 a year? Get the good stuff, and use it.

▸ Work hard on your letterhead and logo. Embossed letterhead with a professional logo will not only enhance your image, it might also speed collections. So spend some money on a graphic artist to develop a logo that conveys the image you want.

▸ The letter must be brief, to the point, and worded properly. Misspelled words, especially in the era of spell checks, are suicide.

▸ The words "new" and "free" will attract attention. There is not much you can call "free," but you can invent almost anything that is "new."

▸ Letters of introduction from former clients are good because you will seldom, if ever, sell your services with the marketing letter alone. Letters of introduction will buy you face time, and face time—making an impression, establishing rapport, and building confidence—is what wins clients.

▸ Give price parameters, not exact amounts. Every case is different, as is every client. Your fees can vary widely depending on location, requirements of the assignment, difficulty of the investigation, and so on. Don't trap yourself into fees that are too low. On the other hand, don't scare off a client with sticker shock.

▸ Direct mailing is like any kind of advertising—it requires repetitiveness and constant reinforcement. Think up ways to do repeat mailings without getting redundant. I got a tremendous amount of business with whimsical, custom-made Christmas cards.

Clients loved them and often kept them on bulletin boards, but I had to invent more and more clever ideas every year.

▸ A newsletter with informative security and investigative tips and stories of your successes is an excellent way to keep existing clients and get new ones. I once gave the phone numbers of former KGB officers for hire. No one hired any, but it was a great attention grabber.

Make direct mailings a part of your regular business routine. It keeps your name in the frontal lobes of your former clients, informs your client base of any new services you offer, trumpets your successes, and generates new prospects. Be creative. Even ordinary business announcements (e.g., moving to better offices, hiring a new investigator) are good excuses to get your name out there in an inoffensive manner.

PLAYING THE GOOD SAMARITAN

Most people go through life seeing only a small portion of what is around them, but a good investigator does not have this tunnel vision. Years ago, I worked to train myself to observe as much as possible and to constantly ask myself questions of what I was seeing. For example, if I saw a person emerge from an office building carrying a package, I asked myself who the person was and what could be in the package. It forced me to notice descriptions, mannerisms, attire, and other details. If you work on this, you will see much more than does the average person. I don't remember anytime in the past 20 years where someone I knew saw me before I saw them.

How does this translate into marketing? When you see a lot of things, you get the extra information that can land you clients. For example, a privately owned vehicle parked near a loading dock at an unusual time may be valuable information to the dock owner. Call the proper person in charge of that dock and pass on the information. If you are buying something and see the cashier clip the sale, pass it on to the owner. Do this as a Good Samaritan and not as a sales call. If the information is received with interest, politely ask if it would be okay to send a brochure or business card. I often got new clients with things I saw while on surveillance for an old client, so keep your eyes open for details that can translate into opportunities.

Never compromise your professionalism to get a client. It will hurt you in the long run. I knew a PI in New York who would ask a bartender for change for a dollar. After the bartender rang up a no sale to make change like a nice guy, the PI would wait 10 minutes, then call the owner or manager and tell him that he saw the bartender make a transaction, collect money for it, then ring up a "no sale." He would follow up with another call suggesting he start "spotting" the bartenders. Many times the now paranoid owner would hire him to do so. Not only is this highly unethical, it cheapens the overall profession.

REFERRALS

I basically built my business on referrals. If you do a good job for a client, never hesitate to ask if he or she knows of anyone else who could use your services. Don't hesitate to use the first client's name when following up on these leads. Ask for that letter of introduction, and send it to the lead along with a request to get together and discuss your services.

Word of mouth is the best advertising you can get. A PI's credibility is crucial, and if you can get someone to vouch for you, you are more than halfway home. People generally like to help their friends, so if you score well with someone, he'll most likely mention you to his circle of contacts. The bottom line is that your reputation is probably your most important asset. So build it. And use it.

YELLOW PAGES

If you are concentrating on domestic cases, use the Yellow Pages. If not, don't waste your money. Companies rarely if ever search the Yellow Pages for investigative services; they rely on referrals and reputation instead. On the other hand, people, particularly desperate people, will let their fingers do the walking to find a PI. Without the Yellow Pages, you will get few domestic cases.

YOUR WEB SITE

A Web site is mandatory for a PI who is aiming for success. The Internet is jammed with sites for investigative agencies and, as such, it is difficult to get business from the site unless you spend serious money to make a dazzler or to get at the head of the line in the search engines. What the Web site does give you, however, is credibility. Today, any individual or company considering using you will almost assuredly search for you on the Web. If you are not there, you are immediately considered suspect or, at least, a lightweight.

A Web site needs certain features in order to be effective. First, make sure it is interactive. Examples include letting people apply for a job or ask you questions. List your affiliations, your lead clients if they will allow it, the services you provide, and the geography you cover. Insert a short mission statement in the beginning that emphasizes integrity and service to clients, something like, "We are dedicated to gathering the intelligence necessary for sound decisions and to rectifying existing problems, representing our clients with integrity and commitment to service."

MEDIA ADVERTISING

We've run ads in newsletters, magazines, trade papers, lawyers' journals, and other places where our company name could be put in front of potential clients. Some of these ads were slick, sharp, and expensive. Did we receive a positive return on investment? No. Did we get some business? Yes.

When I say return on investment, I mean whether we received more business revenue than the ad cost. It's easy to become blinded by return on investment issues, but there is an additional intangible benefit to advertising: name recognition. While impossible to measure, there undoubtedly is good benefit to getting your name and agency out in front of the right people.

If you are considering spending money on media advertising, always keep these three rules in mind:

▸ Narrow your target. Advertise in trade journals specific to the service you are trying to sell. For instance, if you are looking for background investigation business, look for magazines that cater to human resource professionals. If you provide investigations to retailers, look for retail trade magazines and loss-prevention journals.

▸ You must be repetitive. Attention spans these days can be measured in nanoseconds. If you are considering an ad in, say, a lawyers' journal, make sure you're prepared to run the ad (or a variation of it) several times in succession.

▸ Business-to-business media is a hard sell. I've found radio ads to yield little or no results. I believe businessmen don't listen to radio spots for other companies the way individual consumers do, so these business-to-business ads generally fall on deaf ears.

PROFESSIONAL ORGANIZATIONS

Again, we're talking the Rotary Club, Jaycees, Chamber of Commerce—the list goes on and on. Join as many as you can bear. Shake hands, introduce yourself, hand out business cards. Offer to give talks or seminars. Be professional; be out there.

THINGS THAT DON'T WORK

Over the years, I've tried practically everything to market my business. One thing that I know doesn't work is trying to advertise business to consumer—that is, trying to target a market of individual consumers rather than companies. I once gave away free service through a contest on a hip radio station, and the guy who won wanted us to follow some girl he liked. Basically, he tried to hire us as a stalker.

I tried a program I called "Check-A-Mate." This was before they tightened up access to credit reports. The idea was to sell background checks so people could learn more about someone they were, or thinking of, dating. I mostly got women asking how much money the guy had or if he had AIDS (after the fact). Sounded great on paper; didn't work in real life.

Magazine advertising has been a mixed bag for me. The ads tend to be very expensive and have limited impact for the little guy; large companies fare better because for them, it's more about name recognition than trying to sell something. So wait until you're big enough to afford magazine advertising strictly for its promotional value before spending the farm on it.

Whatever combination you choose, commit yourself to an ongoing marketing effort. In the beginning, my profit and losses fluctuated from month to month. One month I would have client lunches, send letters, make phone calls, and do whatever I could to get business. The next month I would do the investigating, letting the sales and marketing go stagnant. I was on the hamster wheel for years until I started to market more consistently. The business has to flow in; getting the job done is easier than getting the job in the first place. Once you are established, you can spend more time schmoozing, doing talks, playing golf, and working the cases that you want, leaving the ones you don't want to other investigators on your staff. The real successful PIs do little investigative work; they supervise and get the business. Again, high profile is the name of the game.

THE SUCCESSFUL PRIVATE EYE

The evolution of a successful PI or agency runs pretty much as follows:

▸ Decide you want to be, and have what it takes to be, a good PI: the attention to detail, the logical thinking, the innate sense of adventure. If this isn't the easy part, then perhaps you've picked the wrong profession.
▸ Check with the Department of State or Department of Public Safety in your state for licensing requirements. You may not even qualify or may need more experience. Sometimes this is not so easy.
▸ Figure out the area of investigation on which you wish to focus. It can be a couple of disciplines, but not so many that you do not have a clear identity. Make sure you work at what you are best at, and don't spread yourself too thin.

▶ Obtain your license and insurance, then your basic equipment. Get a telephone line and a good cell phone. Design and order your stationery and business cards. Set up your computer, Internet service, and e-mail.

▶ Figure out how you are going to get a client. Yellow Pages? Referrals? The first ones are the hardest. Marketing and promotion never stop.

▶ Do a case. It can be anything. When I first started, I hid in booths with two-way mirrors in convenience stores to catch the clerks clipping sales. I then questioned them to get statements of admission. I got up at three in the morning to get to the house of a potential worker's comp fraud at the break of dawn. I sat in a car for hours, waiting for someone to take something out the back door of a client's store. Do whatever it takes, but do it well, and charge a fair price. Nothing beats experience in getting and keeping clients. Ask your first clients for referrals to others.

▶ Introduce yourself to the local law enforcement people and pledge your support in every way. Be as professional as possible. Don't try to upstage them, and don't act like you're better than they are—they don't think so. Also, remember that most cops are thinking ahead to their retirement, and many will be interested and even anxious to become private eyes. When the time is right, it wouldn't hurt to throw out something like, "Former police officers make the best PIs, and I'm always looking for good guys to partner with."

▶ Send out marketing direct mailings and press releases with your and your agency's name. Sign up for as many professional organizations and associations that you can. Go to every damn breakfast and luncheon.

▶ Take great care in choosing your location. Is the money you save working out of your home pennywise and pound-foolish?

▶ Consider adding another service that is compatible with your original service. For example, if you are doing domestics, how about insurance claims as well? Or if you are doing mystery shops, add on pre-employment screenings.

▸ As your business grows, weigh the costs and benefits of adding staff, whether it's clerical help or extra investigators.

If you are good, if you work hard, if you have the talent and the personality, if you are in the right market with the right service, and if you stay at it (and if you do not have a nervous breakdown), you will be successful. How successful depends mainly on you and how much you want it (plus some luck).

However successful you end up being, you will most likely have a great ride, never be bored, and do things like you read about in books and see in the movies.

Good luck.

Ch apter 12

A Couple of War Stories

Although sitting around telling war stories is an occupational hazard for struggling PIs, the stories themselves are a perk of the profession. Let's face it: it's gratifying to relive your successes, and some episodes are too good not to tell to others. Here are a couple of my favorites.

HANDS-ON MANAGEMENT

A fast-food restaurant chain in a nearby city was experiencing high food costs, unexplained shortages, and lower sales. Suspecting internal theft, management asked my agency to investigate.

Our solution was to send two video experts to the property, where they surreptitiously installed several covert cameras in the dead of night. They integrated the point-of-sale software from the cash registers with the cameras so the amounts being rung up by the cashiers appeared on the video image. Thus, not only could we see the customer and food items, we could also see what was being rung into the registers.

We then remotely accessed the system from our offices in Boston and watched. It did not take long for us to realize that the general manager was taking advantage of his position. Registers were being cleared early, creating large overages in cash that subsequently disappeared, and large-function sales were going south.

We also noticed a whole other range of bad things with this guy, including a hot little affair with a hot little employee.

Armed with incriminating video clips and a determined attitude, I went to the restaurant and, because they did fresh baking very early, quietly went into the manager's office at around 4:00 A.M. and waited. About a half hour later, in he comes, ready for another day . . . and not ready for me. A short interview later, I had a written, signed statement admitting to some $240,000 in theft through a variety of means.

I called the local police (I had made contact earlier), who arrived a couple of minutes later. They read his statement, watched my video, and slapped the cuffs on the perp. The prosecution was a slam dunk, and restitution is being paid. The case was started and completed within three weeks.

IT'S NEVER TOO LATE

An attorney friend called and referred a client to us for a domestic matter. With his referral, we took on the case when she called.

The caller said that she lived in upstate New York and knew her husband was having an affair. She also knew that her wandering spouse was going on a little road trip with his honey and in fact had left minutes before, heading for a motel on the north shore of Boston. She wanted a video of him and her entering the hotel.

Knowing that a drive from there to here would take several hours, I knew we had time to set up a static surveillance at the motel and even knew of several easy vantage points.

"Please give me a description of your husband," I asked.

"It's easy. You can recognize him by his walker," she replied.

Pause. "Walker? How old is your husband?"

"Eighty-four."

Pause. "How old is the woman?"

"She's a young tart. I bet she's not much more than early 70s."

With a hidden smile, I asked what she planned to do with evidence of this affair. Was she considering divorce?

"No," she said. "We've been married for more than 50 years. No sense in rocking the boat now. I'll just make him suffer."

The trip should have taken the gentleman in question about five hours. I had my guy in place in plenty of time. The subject did not show up for almost seven hours. I had this image of him driving on the turnpike at 40 miles an hour with his blinker on the whole way.

Bill, the surveillance man, rolled into the office with a grin.

"Get a good shot?" I asked.

"Yep," he replied. "Hard to miss. Took him almost 10 minutes to get from the car to the front desk. God knows how he's going to hold up with his hottie. Gives me new hope."

I sent a bill for five hours of surveillance along with the video. I was paid within days. Never did hear how badly the old man suffered, but he was a hero with the guys in our office for the next month.

Appendix A
Sample
Narrative
Report

INVESTIGATIONS
MYSTERY SHOPPING
EMPLOYMENT SCREENINGS
CORPORATE UNDERCOVER
TECHNICAL SERVICES
LOSS PREVENTION CONSULTING

DATA QUEST LTD.

CORPORATE HEADQUARTERS
667 BOYLSTON STREET
BOSTON, MA 02116 USA
(617) 437-0030 • (800) 292-9797
FAX (617) 437-0034 • (877) 362-7272
WWW.DATAQUESTONLINE.COM

Company XYZ
Anytown, USA
File No. 100-03-6244
Investigator No. 1153
Corporate Undercover Report
Week Ending Saturday, August 2, 2003

The following report details information gathered during an internal investigation conducted at Company XYZ located in Anytown, USA, by Data Quest, Ltd., for the week ending Saturday, August 2, 2003.

This report is for the exclusive use of Company XYZ management personnel and is highly sensitive and confidential in nature.

(***SAMPLE REPORT***)(Editor's note: This was an actual report for an Undercover Operation conducted in 2003. The names have been changed, and the client's company name has been removed. To help the reader, it should be noted that this investigation took place in the warehouse of a liquor distributor.)

SUMMARY & RECOMMENDATIONS:

- The investigator worked on Tuesday, July 29, 2003, Thursday, July 31, 2003 and Friday, August 1, 2003. A detailed narrative report for each day is enclosed.

- Several employees appear to be stealing alcohol from the client location. STEVE, DAN, TIVON and BIF have been observed to steal bottles of liquor from the client location. Other employees may be involved as well. The investigator will attempt to develop this further. The investigator would recommend a parking lot "sting" operation, or exit search of employees be considered. Data Quest Ltd. management personnel will coordinate and conduct as advised and deemed appropriate.

- Several employees appear to be involved with narcotics, at the very least on a recreational basis. STEVE, FRANK and TIVON all spoke of having the ability to easily obtain narcotics, and seemed willing to distribute or share with others. DAN and LYNE both implied that they have smoked marijuana while working at the client location. STEVE boasted that he had marijuana in his pocket while he was working. DAN and BIF implied that they each had previously stolen alcohol and consumed alcoholic beverages while working at the client location. The investigator also notes that DAN frequently operates a forklift. The investigator noted that this could present a safety issue and will monitor this closely.

- FRANK appears to be willing to distribute guns to other client location employees. The investigator will monitor this closely and will attempt to develop this further.

- Employees appear to be taking longer breaks than the time allotted. This appears to be prevalent during the lunch break.

The results of this investigation for the week ending August 2, 2003 are as follows:

110

TUESDAY, JULY 29, 2003

On the above captioned date, an undercover investigation was initiated at Company XYZ located in Anytown, USA.

The purpose of this investigation is to obtain information pertaining to client interests.

The results of the surveillance appear below in chronological order:

At 9:54 AM, the investigator entered the client location and filled out the time card. The investigator then proceeded to the warehouse office.

Upon arrival the investigator stood with several other employees. The investigator conversed with STEVE (w/m, short dark hair, with facial hair on the chin, and dark eyes, medium build approximately 6'2", 22 years, tribal tattoo on right hand ring finer, tattoo saying "Kristen" with a date in 2001 on left forearm). During this time CHRIS (w/m, short brown hair, medium build, approximately 5'7") checked the employees to make sure they were on time. CHRIS selected six (6) employees and brought them over to an area in the warehouse where the task was to unpack pallets and organize the alcoholic beverages. CHRIS also sent three (3) other employees to work on the forklifts.

From 10:30 AM through 12:00 PM, the employees in the small group performed the tasks. The investigator conversed with STEVE about subject matter not pertaining to this investigation. Also during this time the investigator conversed with DAN (w/m, short dirty blond hair, blue eyes, with a beard, approximately 6'3"), and TOM (b/m, brown eyes, black hair corn rolled, silver chain with a ring on it).

During this time the investigator discovered that TOM had been working for the client location for a few months and had demonstrated good leadership skills and a great sense of efficiency. TOM demonstrated to the newer employees how to complete tasks more efficiently. The investigator observed that TOM operated a forklift and worked with the group to help expedite the process. Also during this time the investigator guided a new employee, JIMMY (b/m, brown eyes, black hair, Haitian, 26 years, 6'2", 175 pounds, small muscular build).

At 12:00 PM, CHRIS stopped over to the area to check on the progress of the employees. CHRIS observed JIMMY sitting down on a case of wine, while the other employees were hard at work. CHRIS took JIMMY aside and conversed with him. Once CHRIS was finished conversing with JIMMY the investigator asked what happened. JIMMY stated, "*he* (CHRIS) *just told me about the break policy.*"

At 12:02 PM, CHRIS asked what time it was, and then told the group to go on break.

At 12:03 PM through 12:15 PM, the investigator sat in the outdoor employee lounge with the remainder of the employees.

From 12:15 PM through 3:00 PM, the investigator resumed work. During this time the investigator conversed with TIVON (w/m, short dark hair, dark eyes, medium build, 5'7" 19 years old, wearing black jean shorts, and a white t-shirt, tattoo on the left forearm stating "life" but when reversed said "death", tattoo on the left shoulder of a cross with a star of David in the middle of it). The investigator conversed with JIMMY and TIVON about marijuana. JIMMY and TIVON were discussing prices of marijuana. JIMMY and TIVON were discussing a possible sale of narcotics. In order to further develop the investigator's cover, the investigator casually inquired about the price of a quarter of an ounce of marijuana. TIVON quickly responded, "$100." TIVON later stated, "*Anything you want, I have sold ounces in the past.*"

During this time STEVE then began conversing about smoking marijuana stating, "*the first thing I did on my way out of here* (client location) *after taking the drug test was blaze in my car on the way out of the parking lot*" (it should be noted that "blaze" is a term commonly used when referring to smoking marijuana).

Using advised pretext, the investigator carefully asked DAN and LYNE (ethnicity unknown/male, 21 years old, dark hair and dark eyes, wearing a white shirt and blue jeans) if they had been smoking marijuana that day. DAN and LYNE responded that they normally would have, but did not have any marijuana at that time. DAN and LYNE then mentioned that their friend (name and description unknown) would be in at 2:00 PM. It appears that this individual is a client location employee. The investigator will attempt to develop this further.

At this time the investigator also conversed with BIF. BIF stated that the other day when he worked, another employee (name and description unknown) was sitting over (pointing to) behind a pallet and was consuming an alcoholic beverage in plain sight. BIF then asked TOM if CHRIS had ever caught this employee drinking. TOM indicated that the employee had not been caught because there were no surveillance cameras in this area. BIF then stated, "*How did CHRIS not see it, the bottle was sitting right over there in front on the pallet CHRIS was walking around?*"

113

DAN then asked, "*Since there are no cameras back here, does anybody ever steal stuff?*" TOM said, "*Yeah, they caught somebody taking a whole liter the other day, the security lady was like 'Do you think I am Dumb' and she busted him.*"

BIF then asked, "*Has anybody ever taken smaller things?*" TOM responded with, "*Yeah probably.*" The investigator carefully asked if they (DAN, TOM and BIF) had ever stolen merchandise. BIF responded stating, "*Yeah, have you seen the flasks?*" The investigator suspects these employees were referring to pints of alcohol and will attempt to develop this further.

From 3:00 PM through 3:30 PM, the investigator punched out for break and proceeded to the designated smoking area outside. TIVON, STEVE and the investigator conversed about subject matter not pertaining to this investigation.

At 3:30 PM, the employees punched back in and waited for the rest of the employees to finish their lunch break before returning to work. The investigator notes that there was no supervision regarding the amount of time set aside for breaks, and that the break policy appears to be frequently abused, as breaks were longer then the allowed time.

From 3:40 PM through 5:15 PM, the employees returned to the work area and finished up the tasks. TIVON began to throw cans of Coors Light towards the trash cage, one can hit the side of the cage and exploded all over another employee. The crew seemed to think this was funny and began to throw cans and bottles into the bin especially when other employees were nearby with the intent of getting them wet from the spraying alcohol.

114

During this time DAN and BIF implied that they each had previously stolen alcohol and consumed alcoholic beverages while working at the client location. The investigator also notes that DAN frequently operates a forklift. The investigator noted that this could present a safety issue and will monitor this closely.

Also during this time PAUL (w/m, dark hair with gray, dark eyes, 5'9" 190 pounds, mid 50's, wearing a white Coors beer polo shirt) came from the breakage area and discussed what items needed to be sent over to the breakage area, and what should be sent to the bottling room. The investigator notes that PAUL'S instructions contradicted what CHRIS had explained to the group.

After conversing with PAUL, TIVON and the investigator walked to the front of the warehouse to locate CHRIS. CHRIS instructed TIVON and the investigator, that PAUL was incorrect and to continue working the way they had originally been instructed to do, by CHRIS.

From 5:30 PM through 5:50 PM, the investigator went on break. During this time the investigator overheard conversations about employees who work in the "bottle room" and that this group of employees had not done any work related tasks that day.

From 5:50 PM through 6:10 PM, the work crew finished up the last pallet, and began to sweep. During this time the investigator observed STEVE and TIVON take some bottles of alcohol off of the belt and tucked it into their pants. STEVE took three (3) bottles of 100 proof (blue label) vodka. TIVON took two (2) bottles of the same vodka.

TIVON stated that DAN and BIF had already successfully stolen alcohol from the warehouse. TIVON the proceeded to say, "*I know one thing, I am going to get drunk tonight.*" The investigator notes that TIVON is 19 years old and not of legal drinking age.

At this time STEVE proceeded to show the investigator where he usually obtained the liquor that he would steal. STEVE grabbed a pint of vodka and concealed this in his sock, underneath his pant leg. STEVE encouraged the investigator to steal as well. The investigator agreed to do so, in order to further develop his cover. The investigator asked STEVE to "*keep an eye out*" and implied that he (the investigator) was going to steal a bottle as well. The investigator took one ½ pint bottle of vodka, and concealed this in his boot. The investigator then walked out of the client location. (This bottle of vodka has been turned into Data Quest, Ltd. management personnel and is being maintained in the evidence locker until it can be returned to the client company.)

At 6:25 PM, the rest of the employees punched out for the workday.

At 6:28 PM, the investigator departed the client location.

THURSDAY, JULY 31, 2003

On the above captioned date, an undercover investigation was initiated at Company XYZ located in Anytown, USA.

The purpose of this investigation is to obtain information pertaining to client interests. The results of the surveillance appear below in chronological order:

At 9:43 AM, the investigator entered the client location and filled out the time card. The investigator then proceeded to the warehouse office.

Upon arrival the investigator stood with the other employees. The investigator conversed with STEVE. SARAH was conducting roll call and directing employees where to go for the day. The investigator was sent with several other employees to the breakage area. The task was to unpack pallets and organize the alcoholic beverages.

From 10:30 AM through 12:00 PM, the employees worked to perform assigned tasks. During this time STEVE and the investigator conversed about the investigator's absence from work on the previous day. STEVE and the other employees were wondering if the investigator had been caught stealing. The investigator explained that there was no work available on Wednesday. (The investigator is a "spare", and is only given work when the warehouse is busy.)

The investigator also conversed with CHRIS and DAN (w/m, short dirty blond hair, blue eyes, with a beard, approximately 6'3"). The investigator notes that CHRIS was working slow and appeared tired. DAN explained that CHRIS was "hung over."

Also during this time the investigator conversed with FRANKY. FRANKY proceeded to inform the investigator that JIMMY had been fired. The investigator asked what happened and FRANK stated, "*JIMMY was sitting down while the rest of us were busting our asses; it was right after the first break, and CHRIS came over to check on us, and caught him sitting around, and fired him right there on the spot.* CHRIS said, (referring to JIMMY) "*we don't want your kind here.*"

At 12:03 PM through 12:15 PM, the investigator went on break.

From 12:15 PM through 3:00 PM, the investigator resumed work.

At 12:55 PM through 1:15 PM, FRANK asked the investigator if he wanted to be certified to work the hand pallet jack. The investigator responded affirmatively.

At 1:15 PM, the investigator was instructed by CHRIS to send the next employee up to be certified. During this time the investigator overheard a conversation between STEVE and FRANK. STEVE told FRANK that he (STEVE) had a "joint" (referring to a marijuana cigarette) in his pocket. STEVE added, "*It is in my pocket half smoked*" (referring to the marijuana cigarette).

During the afternoon the investigator observed that FRANK was being destructive with the cases of alcohol that was going to be sent to breakage. FRANK would throw the cases down with the intent to break them.

118

A short time later ANWARR from the breakage room came over and warned all the employees not to purposely break things, but to simply place them into the cage. After ANWARR left the area, FRANK became angered and stated, "*Who does this guy think he is, he is not our boss? I will show him breakage.*" At this point FRANK took the case he was carrying and threw it down hard in an attempt to break it and create a big mess.

During the morning, FRANK informed the investigator that he had received his forklift certification. FRANK went on to state, "*If that guy ever started with me* (referring to ANWARR), *I would go home and get my piece* (referring to a gun)." FRANK explained to the investigator, "*I got a Glock 9.*" It is unclear if FRANK actually has a gun at his residence.

Later in the conversation FRANK stated, "*I will be getting 7 more guns in a few days.*" FRANK proceeded to say they would be brand new. The investigator asked how FRANK would be acquiring these guns. FRANK stated, "*I have my ways.*" The investigator then inquired as to how much one of the Glocks would cost. FRANK then stated, "*$650.*"

From 3:00 PM through 3:30 PM, the investigator went on break.

From 3:40 PM through 5:15 PM, the investigator and employees returned to work. RAY (w/m, 50's, medium build, wearing Patriot's football hat, white under shirt, and shorts) instructed DAN, STEVE, FRANK, LYNE and the investigator how to label different boxes. FRANK and the investigator worked as a team looking up the SKU #'s and then labeling the packages and then re-stacking them. During this time STEVE walked over and showed the investigator and FRANK his legs. The investigator observed that around STEVE'S legs were approximately 10 bottles of "nips" on each foot wrapped up in his sock.

From 5:30 PM through 5:50 PM, went on break.

From 5:50 PM through 6:10 PM, the investigator and PATRICK (b/m, 21, medium to large build, new employee) finished up the last pallet. During this time the investigator observed that the other employees had begun to sweep.

Also during this time the investigator observed that FRANK was working on the same pallet and kept on departing the area to go and check on his "stash" (a pint of Hennessy Whiskey).

PATRICK stated that he asked about FRANK supplying "purple haze" (a high quality type of marijuana) to PATRICK. PATRICK told FRANK "*I want to see it and try it*" before making a purchase. FRANK told PATRICK "*I'll smoke you up*" (implying that both employees would smoke marijuana, but FRANK would provide the marijuana at no charge).

The investigator observed at the end of the shift FRANK and STEVE both stole the aforementioned alcohol and departed the client location.

At 6:25 PM, the rest of the employees punched out for the workday.

At 6:28 PM, the investigator departed the client location.

FRIDAY, AUGUST 1, 2003

On the above captioned date, an undercover investigation was initiated at Company XYZ located in Anytown, USA.

The purpose of this investigation is to obtain information pertaining to client interests. The results of the surveillance appear below in chronological order:

At 9:43 AM, the investigator entered the building and filled out the time card. The investigator then proceeded to the warehouse office. Upon arrival the investigator stood with the other employees. The investigator conversed with STEVE. STEVE implied he was very "hung over", and indicated that he did not go to bed until 430 AM. The investigator, STEVE, FRANK, and TJ (B/M, 21, medium to large build) were all sent to work in the breakage area.

STEVE and FRANK were throwing cases into the cage; by doing this, the un-broken bottles in the boxes were shattering.

At 10:45 AM, four (4) men came down to the breakage area. TODD (W/M, 6'2", average build, short brown hair, Vice President of Operations) stated, "*I heard bottles break one after another, and I had to come and see what was going on.*" TODD and the other men, were questioning the employees about how the job was done in this particular area, then asked why there was such a big mess, and why there were so many bottles breaking. STEVE spoke, and answered the questions, and explained the process of how the work is performed and what the actual job is. (The investigator notes that employees have been warned on numerous occasions, to carefully place the boxes cage and not to break additional product.)

From 11:00 AM through 12:00 PM, the employees in the small group performed the tasks. The investigator, TIM and STEVE all began to label the unmarked packages while the other workers began a different project. During this time TODD, asked for an extra pair of gloves, and began to work with the other employees, in an attempt to re-package some of the broken boxes and bottles.

From 12:03 PM through 12:15 PM, the investigator rested in the outdoor employee lounge with the other employees.

From 12:15 PM through 3:00 PM, the investigator returned to work.

The investigator then began to work on labeling cases again, until the investigator was presented with the opportunity to become certified to operate a forklift. The investigator proceeded to the truck gate 27 where he was to be certified. The investigator passed the certification.

From 3:00 PM through 3:40 PM, the investigator punched out for lunch. STEVE and the investigator conversed. The investigator noted once again that this break went longer than the permitted time.

From 3:40 PM through 5:15 PM, TIM, IVAN (W/M, blue eyes, light brown hair, 45yrs 6'1", from Florida, and originally from Poland) and the investigator worked together looking up the SKU #'s and then labeling the packages, and then re-stacking them.

From 5:30 PM through 5:50 PM, the Investigator sat in the lounge with STEVE and FRANK. The investigator conversed with FRANK regarding marijuana. STEVE overheard the conversation, and stated he (STEVE) could get anything the investigator wanted. STEVE stated, "*All I have to do is make a few phone calls.*" The investigator later conversed with FRANK regarding the sale of guns. The investigator carefully implied that he would be interested in purchasing a gun from FRANK. FRANK indicated that he would let the investigator know what was available. During this time, STEVE was on the phone. STEVE appeared to be conversing with an individual that he (STEVE) obtains marijuana from. At the end of the phone conversation, STEVE stated, "*The kid is up in NH on his way back down from picking up.*" FRANK asked for STEVES phone number, and it appeared as though FRANK planned to purchase narcotics from STEVE.

From 5:50 PM through 6:10 PM, the investigator and FRANK were instructed by CHRIS to move specific pallets to a different location for other employees to work on. FRANK and the investigator worked on this task.

The investigator observed STEVE preparing to leave for the day. STEVE concealed a pint of vodka in his boot and then departed the building.

At 6:25 PM, the rest of the employees punched out for the workday.

At 6:28 PM, the investigator departed the client location.

END OF REPORT

Ap pendix B
Sample
Check-Off
Report

STORE LOCATION:		
DAY & DATE OF AUDIT:		
ENTRANCE TIME:		COMPANY LOGO
EXIT TIME:		
AUDITOR #:		

SCORING SUMMARY	PTS	ACT	%
EXTERIOR APPEARANCE	9	0	0.00
STORE APPEARANCE	7	0	0.00
CUSTOMER SERVICE	8	0	0.00
CHECK OUT	63	0	0.00
MANAGEMENT ACTIVITY	2	0	0.00
TOTAL SCORE	89	0	0.00

EXTERIOR APPEARANCE	YES	NO	N/A	PTS	ACT
Was the parking lot clean and free of debris?				1	0
Was the parking lot well lit?				1	0
Were all vehicles parked in legal parking spaces?				1	0
Was the parking lot void of loiterers?				1	0
Was the dumpster covered and the area clean?				1	0
Was the trash receptacle near the entrance/exit doors empty?				1	0
Was the cigarette receptacle clean?				1	0
Were all advertisements hung straight in the windows?				1	0
Was the façade of the building void of vandalism?				1	0
EXTERIOR APPEARANCE TOTAL POINTS:				9	0

COMMENTS - (Please explain all NO answers or provide details of a job well done.)

Be a Big Time, Big Deal Private Eye

B.	STORE APPEARANCE	YES	NO	N/A	PTS	ACT
1.	Did the store have a clean and organized appearance?				1	0
2.	Was the floor clean and free of debris?				1	0
3.	Were all aisles clear of obstructions and easy to walk up and down?				1	0
4.	Was merchandise well stocked?				1	0
5.	Was merchandise clearly price marked?				1	0
6.	Was merchandise dust free?				1	0
7.	Was merchandise on sale evident?				1	0
	STORE APPEARANCE TOTAL POINTS:				7	0

COMMENTS - (Please explain all NO answers or provide details of a job well done.)

C.	CUSTOMER SERVICE	YES	NO	N/A	PTS	ACT
1.	Was your entrance into the store acknowledged by an employee?				1	0
2.	Were you approached and offered assistance while you browsed? (If not, seek assistance.)				1	0
3.	Were employees observed to offer assistance to other patrons in the store?				1	0
4.	Was the employee able to answer questions regarding merchandise?				1	0
5.	Was the employee comfortable making merchandise recommendations?				1	0
6.	Were all employees involved in work-related activities?				1	0
7.	Were all employees professionally attired and easy to identify?				1	0
8.	Did employees abstain from eating, drinking, smoking and chewing gum while on duty?				1	0
	CUSTOMER SERVICE TOTAL POINTS:				8	0

COMMENTS - (Please explain all NO answers or provide details of a job well done.)

CHECK OUT	YES	NO	N/A	PTS	ACT
1. Was your wait time in line two minutes or less?				2	0
2. Was the check out counter clean and void of unwanted merchandise?				2	0
3. Did the cashier provide a polite greeting?				3	0
4. Did the cashier make eye contact with you?				3	0
5. Did the cashier record/scan all products into the register?				3	0
6. Did the cashier quote the amount due?				3	0
7. Was the amount quoted the same as the amount which displayed on the register dial?				3	0
8. Did the cashier quote the amount tendered?				3	0
9. Did the cashier place the cash payment directly into the cash register drawer?				3	0
10. Did a receipt generate from the register during the transaction?				3	0
11. Was change extracted from the cash register drawer?				3	0
12. Did the cashier count back the amount of change returned?				3	0
13. Was the correct amount of change returned?				3	0
14. Did the cashier close the cash register drawer tightly at the end of the sale?				3	0
15. Was the cash register drawer closed tightly between all observed sales?				3	0
16. Was the register area void of any loose bills or change?				3	0
17. Were proper cash handling procedures followed?				3	0
18. Did the cashier offer you the receipt?				3	0
19. Did the receipt correctly list the product(s) purchased and the price(s) charged?				3	0
20. Was the purchased merchandise placed into a bag?				2	0
21. Did the cashier thank you at the end of the sale?				3	0
22. Was the cashier polite and professional in manner?				3	0
CHECK OUT TOTAL POINTS:				63	0

COMMENTS - (Please explain all NO answers or provide details of a job well done.)

127

Be a Big Time, Big Deal Private Eye

E.	MANAGEMENT ACTIVITY	YES	NO	N/A	PTS	ACT
1.	Did you observe a manager on duty?				1	0
2.	Was the manager involved in work-related activities?				1	0
	MANAGEMENT ACTIVITY TOTAL POINTS:				2	0

COMMENTS - (Please explain all NO answers or provide details of a job well done.)

F. EMPLOYEE DESCRIPTIONS

FLOOR ASSISTANCE

Race		Sex		Age
Hair Color		Length		Height
Build		Glasses		Uniform
Nametag		Other		

CASHIER

Race		Sex		Age
Hair Color		Length		Height
Build		Glasses		Uniform
Nametag		Other		

MANAGER

Race		Sex		Age
Hair Color		Length		Height
Build		Glasses		Uniform
Nametag		Other		

OTHER

Race		Sex		Age
Hair Color		Length		Height
Build		Glasses		Uniform
Nametag		Other		

128

G. PURCHASE(S)		
ITEM	PRICE	

RECEIPT #	
SUB TOTAL	
TAX	
TOTAL PAID	

SURVEY PERFORMED BY:

DATA QUEST LTD. - MYSTERY SHOPPING DIVISION

180 LINCOLN STREET, BOSTON, MA 02111

(617) 437-0030; (800) 292-9797 FAX (617) 437-0034

WWW.DATAQUESTONLINE.COM

Appendix C
Sample
Employee Release Form

As noted in Chapter 2, you need a signed release from a job applicant before you can pull his or her credit report for a pre-employment screening. It is not enough to rely on the applicant's signature at the bottom of the job application acknowledging that the position may be contingent on a background check. In order to be in compliance with the Fair Credit Reporting Act, a separate signed form giving you permission to obtain the report is required.

The following page shows a copy of the form my company uses to gain legal access to a job applicant's credit records. As you can see, it authorizes access to a wide range of entities that might have records on the individual.

Note also the separate "employment screening division" we have set up to gain legal access to credit records, as discussed in Chapter 2.

BE A BIG TIME, BIG DEAL PRIVATE EYE

INVESTIGATIONS
MYSTERY SHOPPING
EMPLOYMENT SCREENINGS
CORPORATE UNDERCOVER
TECHNICAL SERVICES
LOSS PREVENTION CONSULTING

DATA QUEST
LTD.

CORPORATE HEADQUARTER
180 LINCOLN STREE
BOSTON, MA 02111-240
(617) 437-0030 • (800) 292-979
FAX (617) 437-0034 • (877) 362-727
WWW.DATAQUESTONLINE.COM

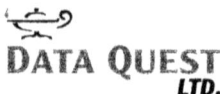

RELEASE AND AUTHORIZATION

I authorize Data Quest Reporting Service, the Employment Screening Division of Data Quest, Ltd., its subsidiaries, affiliates, employees and agents to make inquiry of and request information from, but not limited to, any Individuals, Employers, Education Institutions, Courts, Probation Departments, Law Enforcement & Governmental Agencies (federal, state and local, without exception, both foreign and domestic), Public Agencies, Credit Bureaus, and any other entities that may possess information concerning me or that may be custodians of records relating to me. I also authorize the above described sources to release all information requested, including salary data and subjective evaluations, and I hereby release those sources from any and all liabilit arising out of the release of any such information.

I understand that my prospective employer intends to use the information obtained through the investigation for employment purposes only, and shall not disclose such information to any other party.

I understand that before I am denied employment based upon information in the consumer report, I will be provided with a copy c the report, as well as a description in writing of my rights under the Fair Credit Reporting Act. I also understand if I disagree with the accuracy of any information in the report, I must notify Data Quest Reporting Service - (800) 292-9797 x 119 - within five days of my receipt of the report. If I notify the CRA within five days that I am challenging information in the report, my prospective employer will not make a final decision on my employment status until after I have had the opportunity to address the discrepancy

I hereby consent to this investigation and authorize Data Quest to procure an investigative consumer report on my background an to transmit this information electronically. I understand that this release and authorization form is continuing in nature and that th above listed information can be obtained throughout my tenure with the company. A facsimile, copy, or other reproduction of this release shall be considered to have the full authority and effect as the original signed document.

Name (PLEASE PRINT):_____
FIRST   MIDDLE   LAST

Maiden Name or Alias (IF APPLICABLE):_____

Present Address: _____
STREET ADDRESS

_____
CITY   STATE   ZIP
Previous Addresses for Past 7 Years:

From:
_____ to _____   _____
STREET ADDRESS, CITY, STATE, ZIP
From:
_____ to _____   _____
STREET ADDRESS, CITY, STATE, ZIP

The following information is requested for identifying purposes to ensure accurate record retrieval. Age is not criterion for employment.

Social Security Number:_____-_____-_____   DOB: ____/____/_____

Driver's License #: _____   State Issued: _____

Applicant's Signature:_____   Date:_____

132

Ap pendix D
Online
Investigation
Resources

The following is a sampling of investigative resources, databases, and vendors available online that my company has used to conduct investigations. All information was current at the time of publication, but be aware that these types of companies and services come and go. If a Web site listed below is no longer valid, you shouldn't have much trouble locating a site for a current provider.

Your binder of online investigative resources can be organized in any number of ways, but each entry could include the following information where applicable:

> Company name
> Description of service provided
> Web address
> Your log in or user name
> Your password
> Security question and answer
> Telephone, e-mail, and/or name of contact person
> Billing or cost information
> Notes

BRB Publications
www.brbpub.com
Database of resources for background checks, including links to state and county Web sites.

Confidential Resources
onestopinfo@msn.com (e-mail)
Miscellaneous investigative resources.

Degree Check
www.degreechk.com
Provides education verification, including degrees and attendance.

Gorilla Trace
www.gorillatrace.com
Metasearch engine service for licensed private investigators and other authorized personnel. Searches web sites, images, Usenet newsgroups, blogs, media, and more.

Info Cubic, LLC
http://www.infocubic.net
Pre-employment screening service.

Interment.net
www.interment.net
International cemetery search site.

IRB Search
www.irbsearch.com
Database that includes information on people, addresses, phone numbers, assets, licenses, court documents, employers, and more.

ISPY
i_spy_research@hotmail.com (e-mail)
Criminal and civil searches nationwide, except for South Carolina, Mississippi, and Kansas.

LocatePlus
www.locateplus.com
Database that includes information on people, property, motor vehicle records, courts, corporations, and more.

Master Files
www.masterfiles.com
National directory assistance, Social Security number verifica-

tion, reverse cell phone number lookup, nonpublished numbers, and more.

NAPBS
www.napbs.com
National Association of Background Screeners, with all sorts of resources for employment screenings, Fair Credit Reporting Act information, and more.

National Sex Offender Registry
www.nationalsexoffenderregistry.net
List of sex offenders.

National Student Clearinghouse
www.studentclearinghouse.org
Provides education verification, including degrees and attendance.

PACER
http://pacer.psc.uscourts.gov
Public access service that allows users to obtain case and docket information from federal appellate, district, and bankruptcy courts and from the U.S. Party/Case Index.

PDJ Investigative Resources
www.pdjservices.com
Miscellaneous investigative resources.

Rapid Court
www.rapidcourt.com
Public records, including address histories, criminal records, nationwide sex offender database, security watch list, and more.

Search Systems
www.searchsystems.net
Largest public record directory on the Internet, including access to corporate filings, criminal records, sex offenders, civil court filings, vital records, property records, unclaimed property, professional licenses, and more.

BE A BIG TIME, BIG DEAL PRIVATE EYE

Softech International
www.softechinternational.com
Database for driving and motor vehicle records.

Source Resources
www.sourceresources.com
Miscellaneous investigative resources.

Tracers Info
www.tracersinfo.com
Database with information on people, property, vehicles, courts, corporations, and more.

US Interlink
www.usinterlink.com
Database with information on historic/current addresses, telephone numbers, assets, Social Security number traces, and more.

U.S. Dept. of the Treasury Office of Foreign Assets Control
http://www.ustreas.gov/offices/enforcement/ofac/sdn/
Terrorist watch list.

U.S. Drug Enforcement Administration
www.usdoj.gov/dea/fugitives/fuglist.htm
List of DEA's most wanted fugitives.

U.S. Immigration and Customs Enforcement
www.ice.gov/pi/investigations/wanted/fugitives.htm
List of Customs Department's most wanted fugitives.

U.S. Postal Service
http://zip4.usps.com/zip4/
ZIP code locator by address, city, or company.

The Work Number
www.theworknumber.com
Verifies employment and income information.

About the Author

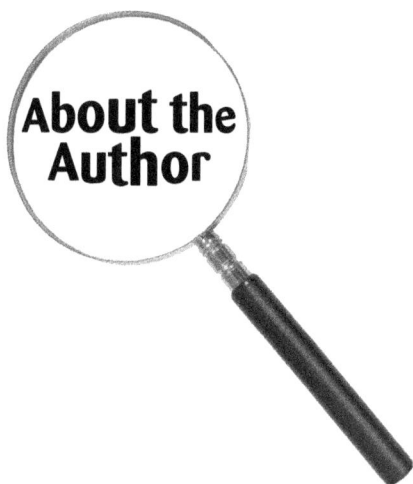

Russ Bubas is the owner of Data Quest, Ltd. Since he founded the company in 1981, Russ has built Data Quest from a small, local detective agency to a successful corporate private investigations firm with international capabilities and a client base of more than 1,000 companies. Data Quest is headquartered in Boston and maintains a branch office in New York City.

Russ's distinguished career of more than 35 years has earned him a reputation as one of the leading investigative experts in the business. His experience includes four years as a U.S. Army counterintelligence officer serving in the United States and Korea, vice president of the Better Service Bureau (New York City), Director of Loss Prevention for R.H. Stearns Company (Boston), and Manager of Investigative Services for the Standard Service Bureau (Boston). He currently acts as the loss-prevention director for a number of companies and provides loss-prevention consultations and seminars to businesses to reduce their shortages and losses.

Russ holds a bachelor's degree in Business Administration from New York University. He is a long-standing member of the American Society for Industrial Security (ASIS) and a frequent contributor to a number of retail and hospitality trade publications. He can be reached through his Web site at www.dataquestonline.com.